The Game Shooting

HANDBOOK

The Game Shooting

HANDBOOK

Mike Barnes
Illustrated by Will Garfit

THE CROWOOD PRESS

First published in 1988
as *The Game Shot* by
The Crowood Press Ltd
Ramsbury, Marlborough
Wiltshire SN8 2HR

www.crowood.com

Revised edition, retitled *The Game Shooting Handbook*,
published in 2005

British Library Cataloguing-in-Publication Data
A catalogue record for this book is available from the
British Library.

ISBN 1 86126 804 1

Typeset by Chippendale Type

Printed and bound in Great Britain by CPI Bath

Contents

Acknowledgements

I am grateful to a number of people who have assisted with this book. I should first and foremost like to thank Will Garfit for his excellent illustrations, many of which first appeared in a series published by *Shooting Times*. Thanks also to John Buckland and David Olive who produced the series. David is the proprietor of Apsley Shooting Grounds near Andover, and is one of the country's finest coaches and a superb shot. I must stress that the words and pointers given in these pages are mine – David is the chap to provide the expert tuition. For the chapter on the history and development of the sporting shotgun I thank David Baker, who is also the author of the definitive books on this subject, *The British Shotgun, Volumes I & II*. And for the cartridges and choke chapter I am indebted to the late David Garrard, for so many years the country's leading authority in this field. There are a number of others to whom I am grateful. Special thanks go to Andrew Atkinson, Peter Collins and the late Philip Grimes, along with the many who have shared their knowledge and enjoyment of the sport with me over the years. All in different ways have made a greater contribution than they possibly realise. Finally, to the two whose patience made it possible – Lynne and Tom.

Introduction

Game shooting is probably the most traditional of all sports. The very act of 'hunting' game is responding to one of man's earliest instincts, and the manner of shooting 'driven' has varied little since the invention of the breechloading shotgun in the middle of the 19th century. But it is an ever changing world in which we live and nothing goes untouched, even shooting.

It would have been close to heresy to have 30 years ago produced a book entitled *The Game Shot* which included chapters on duck, geese and pigeon. Indeed such a notion will still probably be frowned upon in some quarters today. But in the 1980s it would be unrealistic to do otherwise. They are all sportsman's quarry and come well within that invaluable yardstick of never shooting anything that cannot be eaten or isn't vermin (and all of the species included in the following pages are excellent on the table!). 'Game' as such is defined in the Game Act of 1831, and the categories of species included have more or less stayed that way ever since. Shooting really is a very traditional sport.

But each quarry has an undeniable appeal of its own. Pigeon and duck have as much right to inclusion as grouse and pheasant, both offering first class sport, and often calling for hard-earned fieldcraft.

There have been other changes too. Game shooting was once the preserve of the wealthy Victorian aristocracy who accounted for huge bags and recorded vast personal tallies. This exclusivity was gradually eroded and with the spread of the railways and the break-up of many of the big estates, pheasant gained enormous popularity over the length and breadth of the land. The character of the countryside with its woodland, field and hedgerow patchwork was such that even with

modest keepering efforts there were mostly good stocks of both pheasant and partridge. For many years farming fraternities were able to enjoy marvellous sport. Between the wars, during the 1950s and even the 1960s there was excellent wild bird shooting to be had. While on the bigger shoots, labour was cheap and a hardworking team of zealous keepers with a rearing programme and a vendetta against vermin would produce prodigious bags.

Then came the new age of farming. Prairie-like fields, monoculture, intensified land use and the spread of urban sprawl. It probably never entered anyone's head that game populations would be affected by what was taking place – there had always been plenty of pheasants and partridges and there was no reason to assume that this happy state of affairs would ever alter. But by the end of the 1970s it was clear that the glory days of game shooting were gone. Season after disappointing season could no longer be simply attributed to poor weather – there was something clearly amiss.

Taking stock of the countryside offered the answer – there were now few hedgerows for nesting, stubble had become a thing of the past (burned as soon as the combine was finished – scorched earth is no place for young game), ploughs or cutters had removed most rough corners, ditches replaced by underground drainage and pesticides had killed the insects on which young chicks are so dependant. And on top of all of that a widespread and continuing loss of fields to building developments, motorways and public rights of way. With the rising cost of labour and the mechanisation of farms there were also far fewer keepers – and consequently much more vermin everywhere. Added to which there was a growing band of people calling themselves 'environmentalists' who knew little of the ways of the countryside. Their intentions were good but their grasp of nature was more in tune with Walt Disney than the world around them. They were however making a lot of noise and anxious to bring an end to field sports.

It all sounds quite depressing, doesn't it? Yet, ironically, against this backdrop has evolved a sport of shooting which in many ways is healthier than ever. Today's sporting man is concerned about his countryside – he does more for the habitat than almost anyone else. He knows that without the covert, hedgerows, game crops, corners of woodland there would be no game, nor little else. By the very nature of being a harbour for game, a keepered shoot is a haven for all wildlife. It is here where songbirds, butterflies and wild flowers can still be found aplenty.

The general alarming slump in wild bird returns brought about by the changing face of that large (and growing) part of the country-side over which the keeper has no control, has also meant that today's shooting man values his sport and his quarry possibly as never before. Now, more than ever, it's not so much the number of birds shot, but were they 'good' birds? Did they fly well?

It was easy to point a finger of blame at the farmers, but almost anyone in their position would have done the same. In economic terms, they became more efficient. Now most of those farmers who shoot are anxious to do what they can. Millions of trees have been planted during the last 20 years to be enjoyed by future generations. More rough corners and headlands are being left and pesticides sprayed selectively.

Of course, it is still possible to shoot big bags – money can buy most things (that never changes) and a very large percentage of driven shooting is accounted for by commercially-let days or paying syndicate guns. Where once the costs of running a shoot were absorbed by the estate in question, now in the majority of instances the private invitation shoot is a thing of the past. The overheads involved have simply become too high. It is estimated that each reared pheasant presented to the guns costs in the order of £20 – and a return of 40 per cent of birds released is reckoned to be a decent average. Commercial shoots of decent quality charge £25 per bird minimum (and some 20 million are released one way or another each year).

The fact that so many people are paying for their shooting is not necessarily a bad thing. It means that the sport has opened itself and anyone can buy a day to match their pocket, be it walked up, mixed driven of 80–100 or days of 300 and more. There are even a few shoots offering those Victorian skies dark-ened by pheasants. If that's what people want, it's their decision. But most folk nowadays prefer a decent day which offers a few good shots to savour, rather than a large-scale shoot-out (which also provides fodder for Fleet Street).

The cost of any day, incidentally, is not regarded as being spent purely on the shoot-ing – it provides the pleasure of both the anticipation and the memory, which together play such an important part in the enjoyment of all shooting.

What has happened is that game shooting has become accessible to more people than ever before. Many come into the sport with-out the traditional father-to-son 'upbringing' and the inherited gun. But they are anxious to know and through shooting colleagues and the considerable efforts of the Countryside Alliance, Game Conservancy Trust and BASC they are aware of what is expected of them.

But because of their fresh approach they can look at the sport from a fresh vantage point. They don't necessarily do something because that's how it has always been done, but as they see it should be done. The ways of the field, the etiquette and the simple plea-sures to be enjoyed as a result of a disciplined formality are still there. It's good, safe and reassuring that values are upheld.

The modern shooting man is not, however,

If only the guns always performed as well as the beaters!
Anyone who shoots can learn much from a day's beating.

exclusively hooked on driven game. He will also look forward to an evening's flight at duck, a day at the bottom of a hedgerow in front of pigeon decoys and a chance at a goose. And he will also realise that the best gun for all of these different types of shooting does not necessarily have to be a side-by-side. There is no finer gun than the English side-lock, but is it always the right gun for the job, and is it necessary to pay so much for a gun? If so, with big prize-money at stake, why do the top clay pigeon shooters not use one?

The modern sportsman may have fewer birds at which to shoot (depending on circumstances, including pocket and opportunity!) and will therefore look to make the most of his performance. We all make elementary mistakes in the field. We have good days and we have bad days – we have days when a good shot is followed by three bad ones. What is the cause of this? Why is it sometimes difficult to take a clean shot at a hare? Is the redleg partridge a poor sporting proposition and why does a woodcock cause consternation among beaters? It certainly isn't necessary to be a crack shot to enjoy your day but improving your standard will undoubtedly add to your sport. There is nothing worse than a string of misses – it can definitely affect the actual pleasure of 'being there'. Moreover, there is a moral obligation to shoot reasonably well – wherever possible birds should be taken cleanly and well.

I would never claim to be the greatest shot in the world (not by a long way!) nor the finest naturalist. But I have been fortunate over the years to meet some remarkable people. In shooting there is a welcome everywhere you go. I'll swear that some of the nicest people you're ever likely to meet are those who shake your hand on a cold winter's morning before a day's sport gets under way. During my travels as a sporting journalist I have seen some marvellous shooting from the grouse moors of Scotland to the high valley pheasants of Devon; I have shared and enjoyed the fieldcraft of people such as goose guide Alan Murray and pigeon shooter Philip Fussell; and fascinated at the vaults of knowledge stored in the minds and memories of keepers everywhere. I have been given endless hours of pleasure purely by being in the company of such men. In *The Game Shot* I have endeavoured to pass on some of what I have learned. The book is not intended to be either a manual for dead-eye Dicks or a definitive work on all the game species – there are others that specialise in all of these areas.

While born and raised in the country and from an early age keen on most country pursuits, it wasn't until much later that I 'discovered' shooting. I have been fortunate in that in order to write widely on the many aspects of the subject, I have been able to ask questions that I might otherwise have never dared (for not wishing to give away my ignorance). Neither would I have been able to have them answered by so many who knew so much. I am perhaps typical of the new breed of shot that the changes of the last 25 years have brought to our sport. I like to think that what I see and enjoy is the best of both worlds – the old and the new – but never at the expense of tradition.

In a way this book is not written by me – it is the thoughts and experiences of others through my eyes and typewriter. And also through the brushes of artist Will Garfit who has so beautifully captured the sport in all its many guises. I hope you enjoy it.

1 The Sporting Shotgun: A Brief History

by David Baker

INTRODUCTION

The shotgun that we know and use today will appear to many as a relatively simple contrivance. However, this simplicity is more apparent than real and conceals on the one hand the precision needed for the gun to function safely, effectively and for a long, useful life, and on the other the long and vigorous process of research and development which lies behind it.

Guns have been used to fire small shot for more than 500 years, but for the first 200 or more years their standard use was for firing on small animals and birds on the ground or water – prey which had either been stalked or lured into range. Then, some time in the early to mid-seventeenth century, and probably in France, there began a fashion and an admired skill of shooting birds in full flight – 'shooting flying' as it was termed. It is the response of generations of gunmakers to the needs of the sportsman who wished to continue and enhance this skill which produced the shotgun of today.

To begin this story, we therefore have to go back to the guns of the reign of Charles II. The guns of this era were in general single-barrel muzzle-loaders which were stocked almost to the muzzle and fired by a somewhat crude flintlock. They were much longer in the barrel than those we use today, around 40 inches (102 centimetres) being normal. As a result, these guns handle quite unlike a modern gun. Because of their long barrels and lack of central weight concentration, they have much more the character of a broomstick. It is a measure of the leisurely rate of change in the seventeenth and eighteenth centuries that guns essentially of this description remained the standard pattern until the last decade of the eighteenth century. Then, two seemingly trifling innovations sowed the seeds of the modern gun.

The changes were in the design of the breech end of the barrel by which the charge of powder was induced to burn more rapidly. The introduction of granular or 'corned' gunpowder enhanced this process. As a result, the length of the barrel could be reduced to 32 inches (81 centimetres) and the double-barrel gun, from being a ponderous oddity, became an acceptable sporting gun. As with practically every other innovation, be it in gun design or in the wider world, there were 'experts' who considered the change a mistake and double-barrel guns were condemned as both dangerous and unsporting.

Despite the critics, the double-barrel became increasingly popular and, when the speed of ignition was better understood as an important aid to the sportsman, great attention was given to detail improvements of the flintlock. By the early years of the nineteenth century the locks of a high quality sporting gun were marvels of both ingenuity and workmanship, for it was on these that the gunmaker's reputation, in great measure, depended.

Ironically, hardly had these standards been

set when another innovation rendered them obsolete. In 1807, as a result of experiments over a number of years, the Reverend A.J. Forsyth, a sporting minister from Belhelvie in what was then Aberdeenshire, obtained a master patent on the use of the class of chemicals that exploded when struck, to ignite by percussion the propelling charge. The advantages of the new system of ignition were diverse. The most immediate effect was that ignition was even quicker and so shooting flying was even easier. Equally, however, ignition was more certain – no more was the sportsman at the mercy of the state of his flint or the steel frizzen on which the naked sparks were struck. At the same time, the system was far more damp-proof – no longer was it necessary to carry your gun under your coat tails in wet weather.

For the long-term development of the gun, the new mode of ignition was equally important. Because a sharp blow was all that was now needed to fire the charge, the work of the Reverend Forsyth was to make possible the self-contained cartridge, hence the breech-loading gun and thus the diversity of sporting and warlike variants that we have seen, as technical innovation flourished, especially in the latter half of the nineteenth century.

PERCUSSION IGNITION

In the second and third decades of the nineteenth century, percussion ignition was initially applied to muzzle-loading guns, first using loose powder, then in various encapsulated forms which were to culminate in miniature, thimble-like percussion caps, fitted over the open end of the fine tube or nipple that conveyed the flash to the main charge.

With hindsight, we know this to be the ultimate development of the muzzle-loading shotgun and perhaps at this point we should briefly consider how the sportsman used such a gun. In essence, having fired his gun, it was necessary to pour a measured charge of powder down the barrel, followed by a wad, then a charge of shot and finally a wad to retain the shot. The two wads would, of course, have to be forced down with a loading rod carried separately, or a ramrod which was carried on the gun. Finally, a fresh percussion cap had to be put in place, or the priming pan refilled with fine gunpowder if the gun was a flintlock.

To carry and measure the charges, flasks with measures incorporated into their spouts were used for both powder and shot, while dispensers were made for percussion caps. But some used individual containers for powder and shot, while the latter could be made up as cartridges. These contained a charge of shot in a wire-mesh bag with a wad attached, so that the entire unit was rammed into the barrel.

Even with practice, reloading was a slow process and dirty too because the black fouling from inside the bore found its way on to the ramrod, thence to the sportsman's hands

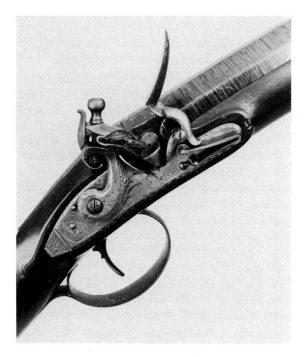

A single barrel flintlock circa *1810.*

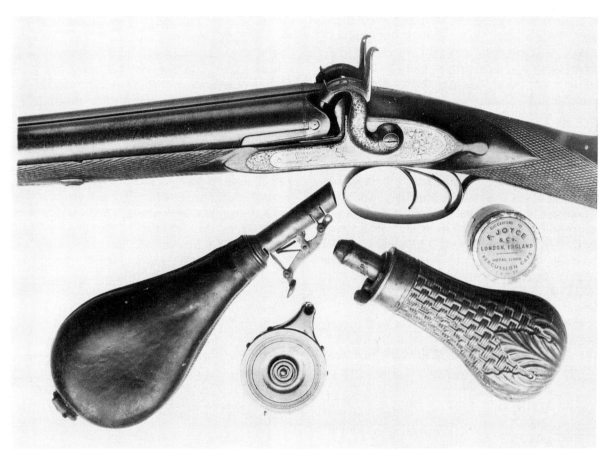

Percussion muzzle loader with powder flask, shotflask, percussion caps and cap dispenser.

and so to everything he touched. Not surprisingly, some of those who could afford to had pairs of guns made and employed a loader who carried all the necessary paraphernalia and handed to his master a loaded gun in exchange for the discharged one.

BREECH-LOADING

Then, as now, the idea of loading an accurately measured and packed, self-contained cartridge from the breech had immense advantages. The guns were firstly speedy, but more importantly safe – no more double charges in one barrel, powder flasks exploding as the charge was being poured, ignited by a

spark in the barrel, or one barrel firing as the other was being loaded and more besides. While the advantages were fully appreciated, their realisation was more difficult. For hundreds of years there had been sporadic attempts at breechloading, usually with replaceable chamber inserts, but none enjoyed wide usage. The problems of cost, fouling and the complication of using a flint and steel ignition proved overwhelming.

Today we know that the answer to all these problems was to be the cartridge, fully self-contained, strong enough to be easily handled and cheap enough to be expendable after use.

Essentially, the shotgun cartridge was a French invention, or more precisely the result

15

of a series of inventions and improvements made in France. The story of the modern cartridge starts with a Swiss ex-artillery man of Napoleon's day called Samuel Johannes Pauly who, very soon after Forsyth, realised the potential that percussion ignition offered and in 1812 obtained patent protection in France for a breech-loading gun and cartridges for it. Both gun and cartridge were important milestones. Superficially, the cartridge bore great resemblance to a modern cartridge with a metal head and a paper case. However, the metal head was solid and contained a depression in the centre of its base into which was compressed loose percussion powder. Moreover, the paper tube was largely destroyed on firing and the system

required the rebuilding of the cartridges on the retained metal head.

By the middle of the nineteenth century, the cartridge had evolved into two practical forms. The first to appear was the pinfire, in which a brass firing pin stuck out radially from the head of the cartridge and was fitted inside a percussion cap internally. The exterior of the head was still metal, but formed from a drawn cup which encased a rolled paper base wad and to which it retained a stout paper tube. The second form was the central fire in which the percussion cap was exposed in the middle of the head of the cartridge. To fire such a cartridge, the gun had to have a firing pin and inside the cap an anvil upon which the percussion powder

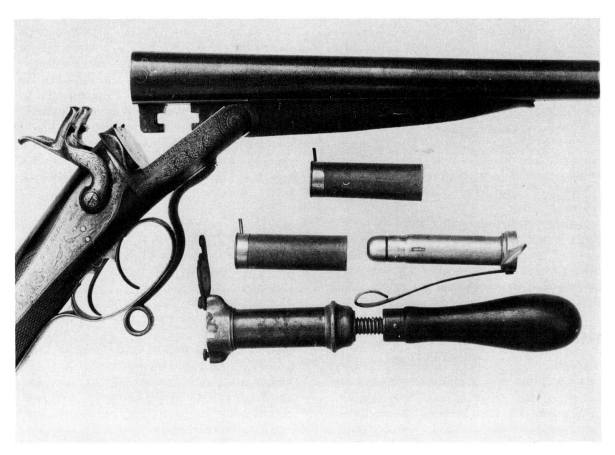

Pinfire gun with cartridges, recapper and turnover tool.

could be crushed to produce its fire.

The resistance that greeted the adoption of breech-loading is scarcely credible today, but the fact is that British sportsmen took a lot of persuading to abandon the percussion muzzle-loader.

It was the pinfire cartridge which first came into use, fired from a gun that was also of French origin. The barrels rotated about a transverse pivot about two inches (five centi-metres) in front of the breech ends. They were held shut by one projection underneath the centre of the barrels which dropped into a slot in the bar that carried the pivot. Into this projection was cut a slot which received a locking bolt. Once more the essentials of the modern gun were evident. The difference was that the locking bolt required the user to turn it shut to retain the barrels. There was also the pinfire cartridge, the pin of which projected upwards through small slots cut in the upper sides of the barrel breeches. To strike these pins, tall hammers with forward projections were fitted to lockwork identical to that on the percussion and flintlock guns.

The story of the rest of the nineteenth century, as far as the shotgun is concerned, is one of perfecting this archetype. The improve-ments occurred in a roughly orderly fashion but unlike in an army, where arms of a standard pattern are issued, used, recalled and replacements provided, the sportsmen were dealing with a host of small gunmakers and both customer and gunmaker had their own ideas. It is also important to realise that shoot-ing was a fashionable pastime amongst all sections of society. In short, gunmaking was a competitive business in which sizeable for-tunes could be and were made. This was the spur that produced not only the technical innovation but also the quality of product blended in a form that has few equals.

The first feature of the gun to be improved was the locking mechanism, which held the barrels securely in place in the firing position. Technically they must be held on to the face of the action. The requirement was not only

to hold them securely but to do this auto-matically as the barrels were returned to their closed position. With these two basic require-ments in mind there were literally hundreds of mechanisms and variants proposed. Spring-loaded catches by the score, working into a bewildering variety of locking sites, above, beside and under, mostly into, but occasionally out of, the barrels. Most of the barrels pivoted open but others swung side-ways or tipped down at the breech, some slid forwards, others were fixed and closed by breech-blocks which slid or swung in every conceivable way. Some varieties were made by the thousand, others by the mere handful; some were no more than prototypes, others never left the drawing board. Out of all this there emerged the supreme idea of having two barrel projections in tandem, 'lumps' to the gunmaker, into each of which was cut a slot or bite, engaged by a catch that slid fore and aft in the body of the gun under the barrels. This set-up is usually called the 'Purdey Bolt' after its patentee, James Purdey, son of the founder of the famous London gunmakers. Typically this bolt came to be worked by a lever on the top of the gun that the user had to push aside to open the gun. On closing, the lumps would cam back the bolt which would snap shut under the influence of a spring.

CENTRE FIRE

At the same time as the snap bolt was being perfected, the central fire cartridge was sup-planting the pinfire. The convenience of the former was that it did not need to be accu-rately positioned in the chamber, which gave it an overwhelming advantage. It was not quite a simple substitution of a built-in firing pin in the gun for a firing pin in the cartridge. The new system brought the more subtle problem that the firing pin could inadver-tently strike the cap at the wrong time and cause, at best, a nasty fright, at worst, a fatality. This problem was greatly alleviated by the use of a spring-loaded retracting firing pin and a clever lock mechanism in which the hammer bounced or 'rebounded' back to a safety position immediately after striking the firing pin.

Even as the central fire hammer gun was perfected by the addition of the rebound lockwork, its successor began to emerge. The so-called 'hammerless' gun, with all its lockwork enclosed within a smooth outline, was certainly not new – examples can be found from the previous century. What was new was that a significant proportion of the gunmakers' customers were now prepared to buy such guns and, in the competitive atmosphere that existed, no gunmaker with a pretence to being progressive could afford to be without such guns to sell.

Once again, many designed their own mechanisms and those who did not sold guns made for them by the makers in Birmingham who built guns for the trade. In the mass of invention, two distinct types of hammerless gun stand out. On the one hand, there were those in which the fall of the barrels worked the mechanism, and on the other those in which some other lever was used. The second category was destined to fade away almost totally and the 'barrel cockers' became the guns of the future – the guns we, over a century later, use and consider ordinary.

Centre fire hammer gun with gun licence for 1883.

ANSON AND DEELEY

There have been a host of barrel cocking designs but few have proved really enduring. The greatest success of all has been the design conceived by John Deeley, the managing director of the gunmakers Westley Richards, and his machine shop foreman, William Anson. In their design, two parallel slots are machined fore and aft in the action body of the gun and the simple mechanism is fitted into these and carried on transverse pivots, the heads of which can be seen on the sides of the action body. This design known as the 'Anson & Deeley boxlock gun', or simply the 'A & D' or 'Boxlock' is cheap to make, strong and reliable. Its main defect is that, to some eyes, it is ugly, square and 'boxy'. Much ingenuity has been expended to mitigate this fault, which also explains why another pattern of hammerless gun has remained popular, albeit almost exclusively in higher grade guns. This is the sidelock, in which the old lock design of the hammer gun, indeed of the flintlock, has been remodelled so as to have its hammers or tumblers fitted inside the lock plate with the necessary provision to cock as the barrels pivot open.

Less common than either the boxlock or the sidelock is what is called the trigger plate

Single barrel Anson & Deeley boxlock.

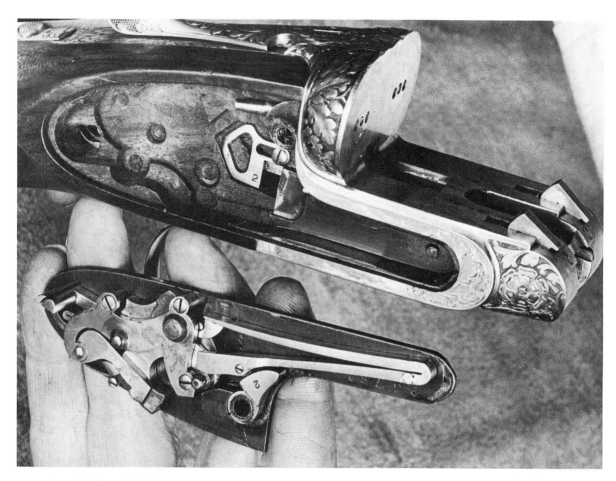

A Purdy sidelock, with lockplates removed.

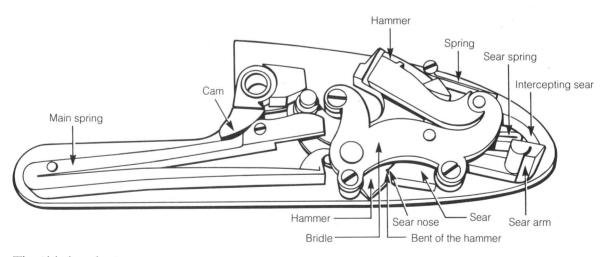

Hammer

Spring

Sear spring

Intercepting sear

Cam

Main spring

Hammer
Bridle

Sear nose
Bent of the hammer

Sear

Sear arm

The sidelock mechanism.

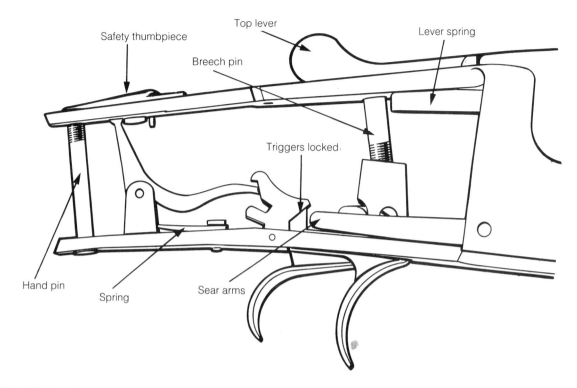

Safety thumbpiece

Top lever

Lever spring

Breech pin

Triggers locked

Hand pin

Spring

Sear arms

The boxlock mechanism.

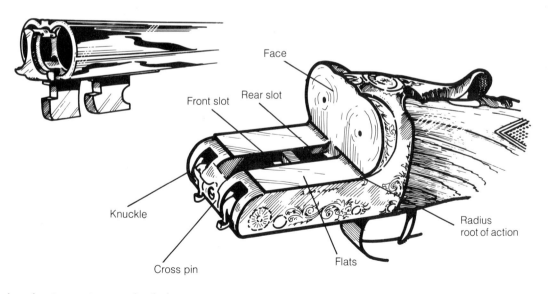

Face

Front slot

Rear slot

Knuckle

Cross pin

Flats

Radius
root of action

Barrels and action receiver on a boxlock.

action. In many ways this can be regarded as a blend of the more common forms, in that it has very much the external looks of the boxlock, albeit in a more rounded form, while the internal work is very similar to the sidelock, but carried on a stouter trigger plate, which often has an upward internal projection.

Nineteenth-century gunmaking was a highly competitive business which had the misfortune to make a product that was extremely durable. Therefore, there was a continual need to produce novelties to tempt customers to buy new guns and, after the perfection of the hammerless gun, this aspect of development became more pronounced. After the 1870s had seen the hammerless gun largely perfected, the 1880s saw the addition of the ejector mechanism, which tossed out the fired case as it was opened. Then the 1890s witnessed the promotion of the single-trigger mechanism which allowed the shooter to discharge both barrels of his gun without altering his grip of the stock.

OVER-UNDER

Another novelty feature was the design in which the two barrels of the gun were arranged one over the other. At its introduction this was an 'under and over' but is now more usually referred to as an 'over-under'.

These began to appear in the first decade of the twentieth century but there were neither the profusion of designs nor the numbers of guns produced compared with either the single-trigger or the ejector. For once this was an innovation which was to be neither fully explored nor exploited by the previously highly innovative British gun trade. In part at least, this was the result of the trauma of the First World War and the subsequent depression which crippled both the gun trade and its customers. These same factors were also to prove a major contributing reason why no popularly priced guns are made in Great Britain today.

The decline of the British gun trade is a huge and complex subject, but it appears that, for whatever reason, no one really invested for the future. Of course, this happened to so much of the industry for which Britain was so famous and has since lost, notably to Japan. And Japan today is one of the countries who supply sporting shotguns to Britain.

The biggest maker today though is Beretta of Italy, who, coincidentally, are the world's oldest gunmakers (founded in 1526). They have a record of massive investment over the years, so that now, with sophisticated technology, they can produce high quality guns at very competitive prices. The precision of their gunmaking is such that parts on guns are totally interchangeable. Together with Browning they were also pioneers of the over-under. John Moses Browning, the legendary American who also invented the famous five-shot semi-automatic, patented the B25 back in 1925. This was the classic boxlock over-under which has changed little in design and is still today in demand and in production.

The famous names of English gunmaking - Purdey, Boss, Holland & Holland, Woodward – all dabbled with over-under design but only in very limited numbers. Beretta, meanwhile, started production of their SO sidelock over-under in 1932 and this gun is also still sold world-wide today (though it remains Beretta's only hand-built gun). They had also patented a mono-bloc mechanism that was to be implemented on all of their mass-production boxlocks.

To underline how much the British gun trade lost out, the output from Beretta alone is 200,000 guns per year (plus 180,000 pistols). The Brescia region accommodates a host of gunmakers of all sizes, specialising almost exclusively in over-under guns. Other well-known names include Perazzi, Franchi and Rizzini, plus highly regarded bespoke makers such as Piotti, Bosis and Fabri. Another country which has provided a lot of guns for the world market is Spain, where in the Basque town of Eibar there is a colony of gunmakers,

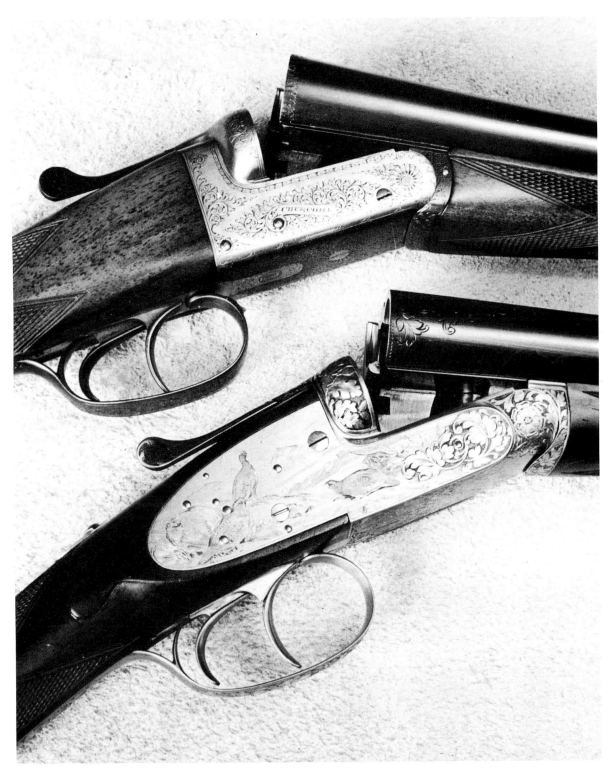

Two of the great names of English gunmaking – Churchill boxlock and Purdey sidelock.

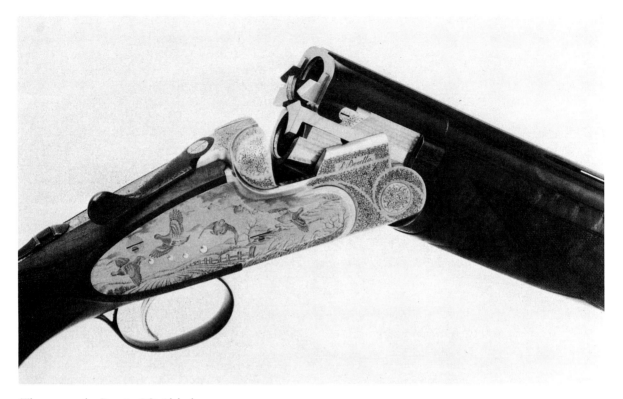

The over-under Beretta SO sidelock.

this time specialising in side-by- side guns. The demise of the Birmingham gun trade presented an opportunity to importers and AYA quickly gained a foothold selling thousands of good, reliable guns at much cheaper prices than anything produced by the English trade.

Sticky times have since hit Eibar as a result of a drastically declining demand for the side-by-side. AYA themselves went bankrupt in the Eighties before joining the government sponsored co-operative Diarm. Happily AYA survived their difficulties and are still making good quality guns, though in small numbers compared to their hey-day. There are still one or two smaller firms in the town specialising in sidelocks who are doing decent business (not forgetting the quality over-under makers Kemen), but it seems that Eibar is experiencing similar problems to those encountered in Birmingham. Browning over-unders are for

the most part now made in Japan (as are Winchesters). However the classic Browning B25 is still handbuilt in Belgium. The other major supplier of the Seventies and Eighties was the USSR where the Baikal was made in huge numbers.

These were reliable but very basic guns and now only relatively few are sold in the UK. The British gun trade meanwhile caters for only very small numbers of high quality guns. The principal makers today are Purdey and Holland & Holland, though Churchills have been given a new lease of life under new ownership and are making bespoke guns for a wider price range. Also to be found in London are other famous names such as William Evans and Boss, still producing top quality guns, along side other smaller bespoke makers such as Asprey, Watson Bros, and Beesley. In Scotland there is Dickson &

MacNaughton, David McKay Brown and Jas Crockart, while scattered around the country are other good makers such as William Powell, Greener and Holloway & Naughton keeping famous names alive with good quality guns. Alas no boxlocks are being made in the UK. The price is too great and the demand too small. This is a story which has taken a lot of twists and turns, and I have, in my brief summary, excluded one of the biggest selling shotguns of all time – the self-loader (or semi-automatic as they are commonly known). Popular in almost every country of the world, they have never been accepted as part of the UK game shooting scene. While nowadays an increasing number are favoured by pigeon shooters and wildfowlers, they are never used for formal game shooting.

Even this superficial sketch conveys something of the complex evolution of the shotgun. Today it is possible to find every phase still in use in various aspects of the sport. There are enthusiasts who dress up in the clothes of 1800 to fire their muzzle-loaders. Early breech-loaders, too, have their adherents who as a rule do not go in for fancy dress. Then there are the later and more modern breech-loaders (including an increasing number of over-unders) being used by game shooters of both the rough and smooth variety.

That brings us more or less up to date. It's a fascinating story, but what of tomorrow? No doubt there are many more twists and turns to come.

2   Which Gun?

SIDE-BY-SIDE OR OVER-UNDER?

The gun which has been generally regarded over the years as the first and only choice for driven game shooting is the sidelock side-by-side. Best English guns from the houses of Purdey and Holland & Holland are famous the world over. While Britain may not have given the world the breech-loading shotgun, it certainly perfected it. But this is by no means the only option for the shooting man. As prices for new English guns go through

It matters little whether your gun is side-by-side or over-under. The important considerations are reliability and gunfit.

the roof, more and more people (in fact, the vast majority) are looking at alternatives.

So what options are available to the shooting man, and how does he choose?

Side-by-Side Sidelocks

These elegant guns are made in limited numbers in Britain, but their price is prohibitive for many sportsmen and the prospective purchaser has to wait over two years for his gun. Obviously only relatively few per year are being made (up to 70 Purdeys, to be sold world-wide) but why does this gun cost so much?

The basic reasons for this are simply stated. A gun such as a Purdey is entirely hand-made, which is very time-consuming. Where once labour was a relatively inexpensive item, nowadays time costs money, particularly a craftsman's time. These guns also feature only the finest quality materials, that is, steel and walnut, which are also at a premium. Then there is the cost of the exquisite engraving which is a hallmark of such guns. And finally the gun is tailor-made for each individual. It is therefore to be expected that the costs will be high, although having visited one or two of the top gunmakers outside Britain I am still unable to grasp why these guns cost so much. Makers such as AYA, Arietta and Garbi in the Northern Spanish town of Eibar produce sidelocks of superb quality. Their very best custom-made models (and they make for the King of Spain) cost less than half of the price of a premier English gun. Even making all sorts of allowances, this sort of difference seems quite staggering.

But again in Purdey's favour is the fact that their guns have been making excellent money in the auction houses. Guns made 50 years ago have been realising close to half the cost

Royale – a Spanish-made sidelock side-by-side by Garbi of Eibar.

of a brand-new model. A pair from the 1980s if sold at auction today could make over £50,000. Clearly if the pocket stretches that far there is much to be said for such an investment and with Purdey's limited output it is to be expected that this situation will remain unchanged.

All of this is equally applicable to Holland & Holland, excellent gunmakers whose guns hold prices every bit as well as Purdey. Second-hand Boss guns have also sold well at auction. But it must be said that the guns which make the best prices are those which have been used the least and kept in the best condition.

Clearly a decision has to be made. It all comes down to budget. An English sidelock is lovely, but a Spanish gun will shoot every bit as well, providing, of course, we are talking about the best of Spain. A terrific number of cheap and inferior guns come into Britain, but despite a sadly declining industry in Spain, the country still has one or two very good makers. There are a few small side-by-side sidelock makers in other parts of the world, but the only guns of note are mostly very expensive.

Side-by-Side Boxlocks

English boxlocks were made in their thousands, with Birmingham the prolific source, supplying virtually every gun shop and hardware store throughout the British Isles. Sadly, no standard boxlocks are made today. The market is still awash, however, with second-hand guns, many of which are dubious buys. The top sidelocks make such good money that it has prompted countless individuals to assume that 'Uncle Charlie's gun must be worth a fortune'.

Many of these old boxlocks are simply past it. They haven't been looked after, wood is often split, actions are loose, barrels are pitted and even out of proof (or close to it). You can, through a reputable shop, still pick up a decent one. For a relatively modest outlay you can buy a gun which may be plain but will

27

give many years' service. Because of the smaller area of metal on the boxlock action (and the fact that it took second ranking to the sidelock) it did not lend itself so well to the skill of the engraver. Consequently, the boxlock tended to be a plainer gun. However, some of the most beautiful guns ever made were the round-bodied Boss and round-action Dickson – the latter is a style of boxlock which is now successfully produced by Glasgow makers McKay Brown (though obviously this is quite an expensive gun).

In the same budget as the standard boxlock, you will find that it is possible to buy an imported sidelock of decent quality. It is impossible for me or anyone else to suggest which is the best buy – it's what suits the individual. Guns don't come cheap, but they are made to last and you are best advised carefully to think through your purchase.

Over-Unders

There is today a third part of the game shooting equation. Rightly or wrongly the over-under has until quite recently never been properly considered as a game shooting gun. Yet in my travels to all manner of shoots throughout the British Isles, some of the best shots have been using guns of this configuration. Of course, I have seen many brilliant shots using side-by-sides and I would not say that the over-under is better than the side-by-side (although no doubt there are those who could put a good case forward to this effect) – I merely point out that there are many excellent shots who favour the over-under, and I am talking about people who do a lot of shooting on some of the finest shoots in the land.

The extraordinary thing is that in virtually every field of commerce and sport, advantage is always taken of technological and design innovation. The Maxply was a brilliant tennis racket, but why do the likes of McEnroe and Becker use large-head graphites? Simply because these newer rackets improve their performance. So why has it taken so long for the driven game shot to accept the over-under?

Indeed there are a number of reasons why this gun has only slowly been accepted:

1. Tradition.
2. It is heavier than a side-by-side.
3. The side-by-side is quicker to reload.
4. The side-by-side is easier to carry on the arm.

There are other reasons too, but mostly personal and without foundation.

The traditional English gun is a side-by-side. The sad fact is that the English gun trade gave the world this beautiful, elegant sporting gun, then sat back and let everyone else get on with it. Attempts were made to produce an over-under by people such as Boss, Woodward and Purdey but they were all looking to make an over-under version of a side-by-side, rather than a new gun. Consequently the end product was a gun which looked quite attractive but was too light and none too easy to shoot effectively (though this is a point on which no doubt some would argue fiercely - and certainly the Woodward 20 bore was a superb gun).

The first successful over-under designs (which have remained in production, virtually unchanged, ever since) were the B25 from American John Moses Browning in 1926 (made by FN in Liege, Belgium) followed by the SO sidelock from Italian makers Beretta in 1932. These two guns led the way.

Though the Browning B25 is still made in Belgium, others in the Browning range are precision made in Japan. Beretta meanwhile invested heavily in the 1960s in high-tec machinery and are now reaping the benefits with mass production, high quality boxlock over-unders at the Brescia factory in Italy. The SO sidelock is still hand-made, however, and as such costs considerably more. As a result of production-line gun-making, the over-under boxlock (of any of the well-known makers –

A Beretta 687 EELL – an Italian-made over-under boxlock with ornately engraved sideplates.

Beretta, Browning, Perazzi, Miroku, Rizzini, Kemen) offers excellent value for money. Consequently, despite our love of the side-by-side, it is thought that over-under sales in the UK now outstrip side-by-side by 50 to one (only 25 years ago it was five to one in the other direction!).

The over-under is certainly heavier than the side-by-side, but this is in its favour rather than to its detriment. English gunmaking became obsessed with light guns. They looked beautiful, and handled superbly in the gunroom, but the field is another matter. While a light gun comes into its own on quick, instinctive shooting such as grouse and partridge, at high pheasant it takes a bow to its heavier brother. Added to which, lighter guns inevitably have more recoil and are not so easy to shoot. Purdeys, it must be remembered, made guns of close to 6¾lb (3kg) – a nice weight.

The side-by-side, by virtue of its construction, has a more accessible gape and is easier to load. But the difference is so marginal that to a regular over-under user it would never be noticeable. Only on very big days would there be an advantage, but this, in any event, would be counteracted by double gunning. Finally, the side-by-side has perhaps a nicer shape for carrying on your arm but the difference is negligible.

The advantage of the over-under is that its

29

extra weight and pointability make it an easier gun to shoot effectively. It is no coincidence that all of our clay shooting champions favour an over-under. While they recognise that a side-by-side is perfect for the straight-driven bird, for all-round shooting and those longer targets they give the vote to the over-under.

How to Choose

So what's it to be – sidelock, boxlock or over-under? The first consideration has to be one of budget. Decide how much you want to spend and then look at your options. But don't make the mistake of buying a very cheap gun – it might look quite similar to a more expensive model, but the difference in price is not there for the fun of it. Because of a lack of consideration given to its design, the cheaper gun will be more difficult to shoot and because of the soft metal used in its working parts, it will also be much more likely to go wrong. This applies to all styles of guns.

I like the side-by-side, but if I know that the shooting will be testing and I want to give a good account of myself I will use an over-under. That may be because I have shot more with an over-under than a side-by-side, or because I find that it suits me better, but I don't think that it's quite as simple as that. Times and attitudes are now changing, but I have in the past been on a number of shoots where I have been the only guest with an over-under. In response to the question as to why I use one, I simply answer that I find it easier. And I also feel that it is easier to make quicker progress with an over-under than a side-by-side. On the average driven game shoot, a side-by-side will always hold its own, and an accomplished shot will always stand head and shoulders above the rest with whatever he is using. It is as an all-rounder that the over-under starts to shine. Its extra weight and pointability are a definite advantage on the more awkward quartering and retreating targets (either taking a shot behind or

walking-up). I personally also appreciate the lack of recoil on an over-under.

Yet there is something undeniably nice about a top quality English gun! Maybe the best option is to buy a best English sidelock for an investment, a good quality Spanish sidelock for some of your shooting and one of the better over-unders for the remainder! However, in an ideal world we would all own three cars, so while buying three guns at once will most likely be out of the question, whatever your decision, remember that the most important part of it all is that the gun must be of decent quality and must fit you (these two factors are far more important than anything else). It is impossible to look smart in a suit that's long in the sleeve or short in the leg, and it's equally impossible to shoot well with a gun that's high in the comb or short in the stock. Having decided which type of gun you favour and how much you want to spend, remember to concentrate your mind on 'gunfit'.

OTHER OPTIONS

20 Bores

We have talked about the different styles of gun on the assumption that we are looking at 12 bores. Here, again, we have other alternatives. More and more game shooters are now using 20 bore. And I personally enjoy shooting a 20 immensely.

I am not a gunsmith, technician nor coach but from personal experience I would say that while the 20 bore side-by-side is a very pretty gun and perfect for driven grouse and partridge, as an all-rounder, the over-under is again the ideal game shooting gun, especially in this gauge. I shot quite a bit with a side-by-side 20 for most of one season some years ago. It was a lovely little gun and I pulled off one or two super shots with it, but I was never able to match the performance which I enjoyed from the 20 bore over-under.

The difference between the two styles was more exaggerated in this gauge than in 12. The over-under 20 is particularly nice as, at 6lb (2.7kg) it has enough weight in relation to its size to maintain a decent swing, while it is also quick, light and, again, lacking in recoil. In my opinion it is the perfect gun for walked-up shooting. It's good, too, on driven sport, coming into its own particularly on those pheasant drives where the pegs are situated in narrow woodland rides. The 20 is a remarkably fast handling gun.

It must be said that I know one excellent shot who used a 20 bore exclusively from getting the gun in his teens until he was in his thirties. This was a side-by-side and his reputation on difficult wild bird shoots was legendary. Again, it's down to the fit of the gun and the style and ability of the man who is pulling the trigger.

While many find that a 20 bore is not their first choice of gun, they come to this gauge at some point in their shooting career and become hooked. It has a pleasure all of its own. It may sound naïve or contrived but there seems more sportsmanship in using a 20 bore. There are certainly few shoots where such a gun is out of its depth – there is little difference between the killing range of a 20 and a 12, and if the birds are so high that they

might be out of range then you shouldn't be shooting them anyway.

16, 28 and 410 Bores

These are three gauges which were once popular but have now fallen out of fashion. The 16 was a favourite for many – slightly lighter than a 12 but more of a gun than the 20. This was the feeling, but perhaps it was *because* it was a half-way house that it ultimately fell from favour. The other important factor is availability of cartridges. You either buy 12 bore or 20 these days – both are mass-produced, though unfortunately this is still not properly reflected in the price of 20 bore loads.

The 28 bore is very much a young lads' and lasses' gun though also enjoying resurgence amongst experienced shots Sir Joseph Nichonson was a 28 bore fan. Useful for starting youngsters nice and early on and especially good for ladies who are desperately worried about recoil. Much the same can be said for the .410, though the 28 is a better bet to start a shooting career.

The naming of the bores, incidentally, dates back to the days of cannon warfare when a Two Pounder fired a two-pound lead ball. So, the size of the sporting shotgun was decided on how many lead balls to the pound

12 or 20 bore? 12 is the standard gauge, but there is much pleasure to be had from the 20 bore.

it held per barrel. If it took 12 balls for the pound, it was a 12 bore, if it was 20 then the gun was a 20 bore – and so on. An exception to this rule is the newer gun in the set, the .410 which is, in fact, an actual bore diameter. The other diameters are 12 bore .729, 16 bore .662, 20 bore .615, 28 bore .550.

Big Bores

The big guns – ten, eight and the mammoth four bore – are for the purist wildfowler. The four bore is only rarely used, but there are still a few tens and eights in regular action on the foreshore, where the lonely fowler will wait in vigil for the magical geese and hope that his extra firepower will pull down a high-flying greylag from the heavens. In actual fact most fowling can be carried out with a standard 12 bore, but there is no denying that the big bores have a fascination all of their own.

Semi-automatics

These are guns which have no place on a driven game shoot. This has far less to do with snobbery than safety. The auto is the world's biggest selling shotgun. Because it is entirely machine-made, utilising a very simple mechanism and few parts, its cost of construction is relatively low. Its short-coming, however, is that on a formal game shoot with a line of guns and an advancing team of beaters, it is almost impossible for others to know whether the gun is loaded or not. At close quarters the open breech clearly indicates that the gun is empty. But it can be very disconcerting at 20 yards. Similarly, when the guns are standing together at the beginning or end of a drive, the sight of an auto can spread unease among the party.

In a clay pigeon shooting situation, where there is a strict code of safety, the auto is absolutely fine. Similarly in a pigeon or duck hide they are particularly good and you don't have the encumbrance of opening the gun to reload in a confined space.

CONCLUSIONS

So there we have it – or almost. Apart from finding a gun that meets your budget and pleases your eye, you will need, most of all, to find a gun with which you can shoot. Providing you follow the loose guidelines of good condition, reputable make and approximate size to match your build this should not prove a problem. But gunfit is very important and obviously you not only need a gun that's right for the job but also right for you. All good gunshops will be able to advise on gunfit, but if you want to prepare yourself properly with some necessary knowledge, turn to Chapter 4.

3 Cartridge and Choke

by David Garrard

THE CARTRIDGE

While it certainly isn't necessary to know everything about cartridge ballistics to be a good shot, it is very useful to have an understanding of your ammunition, how it works and what can reasonably be expected of it.

So what happens when the cartridge is loaded into the gun and the trigger is squeezed? The tumbler strikes the firing pin which in turn indents the capsule of the primer. The friction generated causes the compound to detonate a high pressure, white hot flame which ignites the main powder charge. This burns very rapidly, producing a large volume of hot gases which build up pressure within the cartridge. This pressure, acting on the base of the wadding, starts the charge up the barrel and as the gases continue to evolve it is very rapidly accelerated until it clears the muzzle at around 1,200 to 1,300 feet (336 to 396 metres) per second. This all happens in about one five-thousandth of a second!

The gas pressures compress the case walls and head to the limits of the chamber and the base-wad acts as a gas sealant at the base of the cartridge. The reliability of modern cartridges owes everything to the components used. Powders are mainly double-based, being composed of nitro-cellulose compounds with a proportion of nitro-glycerine. They are very stable and store and perform well under a wide range of temperature and humidity. Burning rates can be accurately controlled.

The primer must match the powder in use (powders vary in ignitability). Modern primers function fully independently of the quality of

the striker blow and being non-corrosive have eliminated the bugbear of barrel corrosion. Gun cleaning is correspondingly simplified. The wadding performs a vital function in sealing off the powder gases from the shot charge. Any leakage can ruin patterns. High quality wadding is essential to good quality ammunition. The quality of most wads today is very good. The biodegradable (felt or vegetable fibre) variety, as often used in game cartridges, produces a more open pattern than the plastic version.

With the one-piece plastic unit in injection-moulded plastic, an over-powder cup seals off the powder gases while the shot pellets, contained in a separate cup, are protected from erosion on the barrel walls. They thus remain closer to their original shape and retain their full weight, both factors making for closer, hard-hitting patterns.

The centre section of the wad acts as a spacer and provides a cushion to the shot charge at one end and the shooter's shoulder at the other. Certainly plastic wads have much going for them and can be relied upon to throw good consistent tight patterns. Some may consider too tight for certain game shooting situations, but this can be balanced by choke.

Velocity and Recoil

The great majority of shotgun cartridges develop an observed velocity over the first 20 yards (18 metres) of flight of 1,040–1,100 feet per second (317–335 metres per second). There is nothing to be gained generally from exceeding these figures. Pellet striking energy

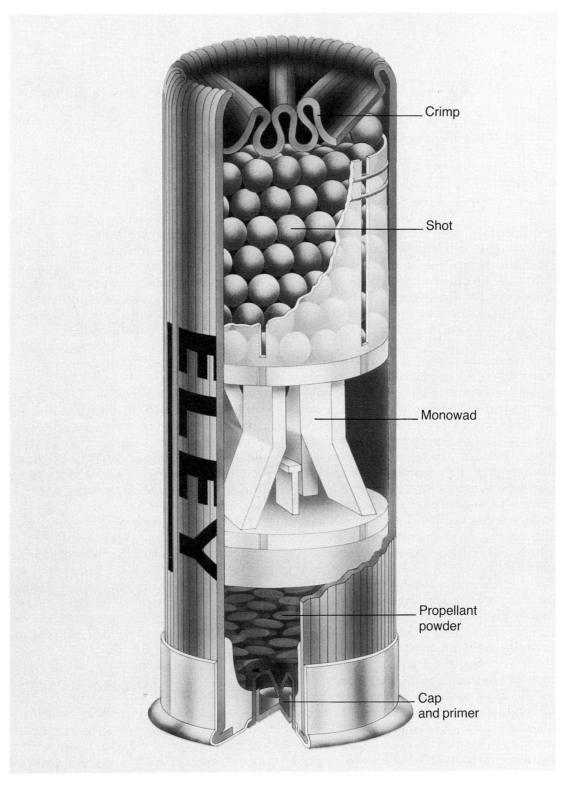

Crimp

Shot

Monowad

Propellant
powder

Cap
and primer

A modern cartridge.

at long range is only marginally increased, but the increased recoil may rise to an unacceptable level.

Recoil is an inescapable feature of all shooting, as the powder gases drive the gun back with the same momentum as they propel the shot charge forward. More velocity equals more recoil, and vice versa.

Excessive recoil is both unpleasant and can seriously affect your shooting. Bruising of the shoulder or face and gun head–ache are the common consequences, plus the disturbance of second barrel shots and flinching. A light gun therefore needs a light load (avoid the HV stuff) and a heavier gun will soak up the recoil and spare the punishment.

Pressures and Safe Limits

It is the pressure generated which imparts velocity to the shot charge. The heavier the charge, the greater the pressure needed for this purpose – the higher the pressure the greater the velocity. But these pressures have to be kept within the safe limits prescribed by the Proof House. All boxes of cartridges should carry information on the proof level of the guns for which they are designed. Always be careful that you do not use a load which will prove excessive for your gun – this can be very dangerous. The following are the guidelines which will be dictated by your gun chamber length:

2½in (65mm) chamber – cartridges not exceeding 2½in (65mm and 67·5mm), 3t/sq in, max. 1⅛oz (850kg/sq cm, max. 32g)
2¾in (70mm) chamber – cartridges not exceeding 2¾in (70mm), 3¼t/sq in, max. 1¼oz (900kg/sq cm, max. 35g)
3in (75mm) chamber – cartridges not exceeding 3in (75mm), 4t/sq in (1,200kg/sq cm – Magnum)

Remember, 3in (75mm) Magnum cartridges are only ever to be used in 3in (75mm) Magnum guns. Eley 2¾in (70mm) Magnum,

1¼oz (35g) cartridges can be used in continental guns proved at 900kg/sq cm. Eley 3in Magnum, 1⅝oz (46g) cartridges can be used only in Continental guns proved at 1,000kg/sq cm.

CHOKE

Experienced game shooters may well think that they cannot do better than rely on the shot loads and degrees of choke that have been evolved over many years in the field by their fellow sportsmen. However, a more rational guide to their choice will appeal to the many newcomers to the sport as well as to those experienced guns who wish to look further than the claims of tradition.

What is Choke?

Choke is a restriction at the muzzle of the shotgun barrel which, acting on the shot-charge as it exits the muzzle causes it to 'print' a denser pattern than from an unchoked barrel. The greater the degree of choke, the denser the resultant pattern. The four main levels of choke, together with the percentage patterns they should produce in a 30-inch (76-centimetre) circle at three ranges are:

Nominal degree of choke and percentage pattern at three ranges

Choke	Range (yards)			Nominal Degree of Choke (thousandths of inch)
	20	30	40	
True cylinder	80%	60%	40%	Nil (*see note*)
Improved cylinder	92%	72%	50%	5
Half choke	100%	83%	60%	20
Full choke	100%	100%	70%	40

Note These figures are quoted as 'nominal' as the actual choke constriction will also depend on other factors such as the profile of the choke section, barrel length, etc. Really short barrels certainly require more constriction than the popular 28 or 30-inch

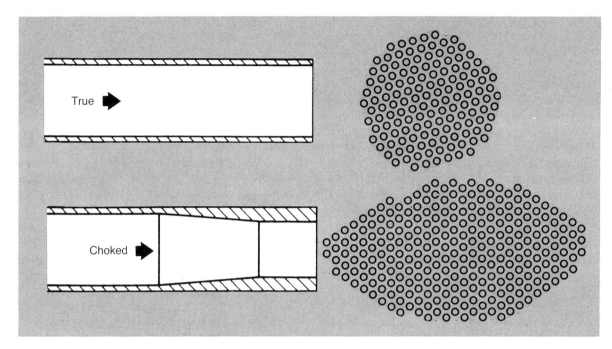

An exaggerated diagram showing how choke works.

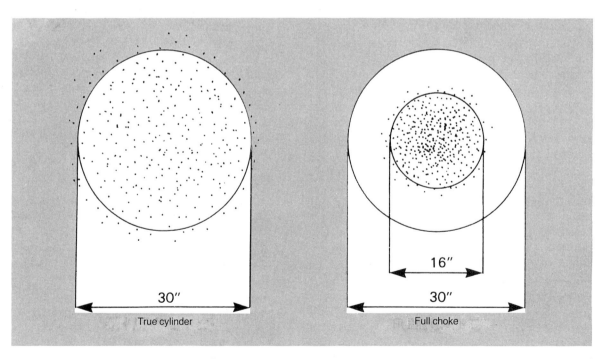

The difference in patterns achieved by different chokes at 25 yards (22.3 metres).

(71 or 76-centimetre) barrels to achieve the same patterns. True cylinder barrels (40 per cent) require a few points of choke, as barrels bored 'straight through' usually print only 30–35 per cent patterns.

To avoid anomalies, the description of choke used in this chapter is defined as the percentage pattern at 40 yards (36.5m) range, irrespective of the actual degree of constriction. On the basis of the figures given, it might be inferred that full choke, with the resultant dense patterns, is the obvious choice for all shooting. So thought sportsmen when choke boring was first perfected something over 100 years ago. They were soon disillusioned, however, and discovered to their surprise that full choke barrels frequently proved less efficient in the field than their 'old' open-bored guns. The reason soon became obvious. The close, full patterns, particularly at the quite short ranges at which game is shot, concentrated the shot charge to such a degree that the resultant patterns allowed little scope to cover the shooters' inevitable aiming errors.

Maximum diameter spread of shot charges at four ranges

Choke	Range (yards)			
	15	20	30	40
True cylinder	26in	32in	44in	58in
Improved cylinder	20in	26in	38in	51in
Half choke	16in	21in	32in	45in
Full choke	12in	16in	27in	40in

This is not to imply that choke boring is of doubtful value to the shooter in the field, far from it. Prior to the development of choke boring, the regulation of barrels was an empirical business of uncertain outcome. The great merit of the technique is that it enables guns to be regulated to produce patterns of predictable density and spread at all levels.

The practical problem is to choose a degree of choke that gives the best compromise between these two factors, taking as our guide the maxim that the best degree of choke

is always the least that will meet the requirements of the sport in hand. To do so involves considering the minimum density of patterns required to make a reasonably certain 'kill' on the usual quarry species. As far as game shooting is concerned these can be divided, for practical purposes, into two groups: the bigger species (pheasants and duck) and the smaller birds (grouse, partridges and pigeons). Most authorities, using a system pioneered by Sir G. Burrard, stipulate a minimum pellet count in the 30in (76-centimetre) circle of 60–80 for the larger birds and 130 pellets for the smaller stuff. These figures, however, do not give sufficient weight to the random distribution of the pellets in individual patterns and the fact that in the thinner patterns, at least, some 30–40 per cent of the 'killing' circle will receive no pellets at all. For this reason, it is more realistic to postulate the rather denser minimum pellet count of 100 for pheasants and duck and 150 for grouse, partridges and pigeons. With this in mind, see the chart overleaf for the patterns produced by some popular game loads at three ranges in barrels bored at four degrees of choke.

The massed figures may seem a formidable proposition but they will stand a little careful study. It is immediately apparent that at 30 yards (27·4 metres) range, a fairly long shot at game, the true cylinder boring produces ample pattern for gamebirds of all sizes combined with a maximum pattern spread. Even at the extreme game range of 40 yards (36·5 metres) the true cylinder barrel in 12 bore prints dense enough patterns for the bigger gamebirds and is close to the mark for the smaller quarry with the 1oz (28g) load of No. 7 shot. Here the 20 bore load is under the minimum value. The improved cylinder patterns, including 20 bore, have a big 'margin' in hand at 30 yards (27·4 metres) and are comfortably dense enough at 40 yards (36·5 metres) range. The half choke patterns have plenty in hand at 40 yards (36·5 metres). This degree of choke is only necessary at greater distances, say up to 45 yards (41·1 metres).

Patterns (pellets in a 30-inch circle) produced by four game loads at three ranges

Choke	20 yards				30 yards				40 yards			
	A	B	C	D	A	B	C	D	A	B	C	D
True cylinder	230	244	272	221	172	183	204	166	115	122	136	110
Improved cylinder	264	280	312	253	207	220	245	199	144	153	170	138
Half choke	287	305	340	276	238	253	282	229	172	183	204	166
Full choke	287	305	340	276	287	305	340	276	201	214	238	193

A: $\frac{1}{16}$ oz No.6 shot (287 pellets), 12 bore
B: $\frac{1}{8}$ oz No. 6 shot (305 pellets), 12 bore
C: 1oz No. 7 shot (340 pellets), 12 bore

D: $1\frac{3}{16}$ oz No. 7 shot (276 pellets), 20 bore
(All with fibre/felt wadding.)

The chart clearly demonstrates the unbalanced features of full choke patterns, excessive pattern density being combined with a minimum of 'spread' and hence of scope for covering aiming errors. It is obviously better that any surplus pellets available should be utilised in increasing the spread rather than adding to the already adequate pattern density. 'Hits' by the fringe pellets can then be scored that otherwise would have been 'misses'.

This evidence points very decisively to open borings as the most effective for game at all ranges up to 40 yards (36·5 metres) or so. If shooting towards this limit predominates, then the improved cylinder barrel reigns supreme, although at the shorter ranges at which 75 per cent of driven shooting takes place, the true cylinder boring would give optimum results. The driven game shooter is therefore advised to opt for improved cylinder boring in both barrels or for true cylinder in the right/under barrel and improved cylinder in the left/upper barrel. Where most of the shooting is walking-up or rough shooting, more choke is advised in the left/upper barrel, half or even three-quarters choke. This arrives at a combination of chokes long recognised as the best for the average gun shooting game in this country.

The theoretical approach outlined here thus comes to exactly the same conclusion as that reached by generations of shooters in the field and should encourage confidence in its wider recommendations. These may be challenged on the grounds that open borings, especially 'true cylinder', carry a reputation for uneven performance with an undue proportion of blown or cartwheel patterns. This was certainly so in the past when the overshot card associated with the 'rolled turnover' closure interfered with the regular release of the shot charge. The universal adoption of the crimp closure for cartridges has eliminated this fault and extensive patterning experience confirms that true and improved cylinder barrels can now print patterns as consistently as those barrels with a marked degree of choke.

Shooters who wish to act on this advice should have the boring of their guns checked by a gunsmith or, better, shoot them for pattern on the 'plate', the only reliable method of establishing the density of the patterns they produce. It is very probable that the chokes of guns other than British-made game guns will require opening up. This can be done easily and cheaply by an experienced gunsmith. It is prudent, particularly with short-barrelled weapons, to proceed with caution, checking patterns at intermediate stages until the boring can be finalised at the correct level. In light of the figures quoted, it is hardly surprising that the multi-choke gun has become so popular, particularly with the all-round shooter.

Minimum Striking Energy

The constituent pellets in an effective pattern must not only be sufficient in number, but must each carry adequate striking energy to ensure lethal penetration of the quarry. Can this factor affect the choice of shot size for game shooting and, indirectly, the degree of choke?

The answer, briefly, is no. A minimum striking energy of 1ft/lb can be assumed as necessary to kill the larger game, while ·85 ft/lb is adequate for the smaller birds. These energies are sustained by No. 6 shot to around 50 yards (45.7 metres) and by No. 7 shot to approaching 45 yards (41.1 metres) range. Thus, the two most popular sizes of shot for game shooting do all that is required at the longest game ranges. There is no need, therefore, to resort to larger shot in heavier loads, fired from heavily choked barrels. This approach is the province of the wildfowler.

GROUND GAME

Hares

These are often shot (if such shooting is not forbidden) around woods in the course of covert shooting with ordinary game loads. The range is usually short, so no problem here. Hares galloping about on the big hare drives in February can present a problem of range which is best solved by self-restraint and by not opening fire at above 35 yards (32 metres). The normal game guns and loads are well up to the job, but here the use of No. 5 or even No. 4 shot is recommended. Duck loads, surplus to the past fowling season, can prove marvellously effective on 'puss'!

Rabbits

These are normally shot, if at all, at pretty short range *en route* to the nearest cover. The most open of the game borings is more than adequate for this purpose. An ounce (28-gram) load should give ample pattern. No. 6 shot is much favoured, but No. 5 puts less lead into the quarry and thus avoids spoiling the flesh.

Woodcock

Most of these are shot with normal game guns and loads in the course of covert shooting. Those fortunate enough to be able to specialise in cock shooting should stick to open borings and the small-sized shot necessary to maintain a minimum pellet count of around 170 pellets in the killing circle. Nothing larger than No. 7 will meet this requirement in normal game loads.

Snipe

By far the smallest target the shooter will ever tackle. Although, like woodcock, plenty are killed with ordinary game loads, specialist snipe shooters should use No. 8 shot in open-bored guns in the hope of attaining a minimum pellet count of 300 in the killing circle.

WILDFOWL

Duck

Duck and goose shooting, indeed shooting over wetlands, now requires the use of non-toxic shot (refer to relevant BASC guidelines for England, Wales and Scotland – they differ slightly). There are a number of options available – steel, tungsten and bismuth. Each have their proponents and critics. Whichever you choose, they are all much more expensive than lead shot, though steel is the cheapest (however it has been on the receiving end of the most criticism, its critics claiming that its excessive hardness results in a tendency of wounding quarry).

Shooting duck at normal range presents no difficult ballistic problem and the loads and chokes recommended for game shooting can be adopted for this purpose. The occasional fowler, who wishes to extend the range of his open-bored gun, should load one of the 'super' 1⅛oz (32g) or 1³⁄₁₆oz (34g) loads. More duck are arguably killed beyond the

Duck loads – patterns at 50 yards (pellets in a 30-inch circle)

Choke	No. 5 shot		No. 4 shot	
	1⅛oz (248 pellets)	1¼oz (275 pellets)	1⅛oz (181 pellets)	1¼oz (212 pellets)
Half choke (40%)	100	112	72	84
Full choke (50%)	124	132	90	106

sea-wall with this loading than with any other 'combination'.

Really long-range duck shooting on the salt-marshes and elsewhere requires the use of heavy loads in well-choked guns. Let us postulate a load to kill at 50 yards (45.7m). The minimum effective pellet count is 100 in the killing circle, each developing a striking energy of at least 1ft/lb. No. 6 shot will just about be enough but it is prudent to use No. 5, or No. 4, both of which have striking energy in hand at 1.36 and 1.97ft/lb respectively at 50 yards (45.7 metres).

An inspection of the chart above indicates that the most effective loads are those using No. 5 shot, preferably 1¼oz (35.6g) in either a half or full choke barrel. This finding, incidentally, is in close accord with extensive American experiments on the same subject. The 1¼oz (35.6g) load has something in hand and would kill, on paper at least, to a yard or two beyond the 50 yard (45.7 metre) mark. Note that No. 4 shot barely attains the minimum pattern density and is best restricted to the heavy, 'magnum' loads in 12 bore, where it should prove very effective indeed. Novice wildfowlers should recognise that even the most lethal combinations of heavy loads in well-choked guns have their limitations and require much practice for effective deployment in the field.

Geese

The huge size of grey geese, double or treble the weight of a mallard, makes them an exceptionally tough, difficult target. An average 'grey' weighing 6–7lb (2.7–3.2kg) requires a minimum pellet count of around 60 pellets in the 30-inch (76-centimetre) circle to ensure a kill. The calculation leading to this conclusion is based on a six pellet strike. The minimum striking energy to ensure penetration of a goose has been widely debated and values of from 1.5–2.5ft/lb have been put forward. The recommendations that follow are based on a figure of 2ft/lb, one that fits in with experience in the field.

These patterns and penetration are easy enough to attain when shooting geese at relatively short range over decoys, say 25–35 yards (22.9–32 metres). No. 3 or 4, or even No. 5 shot will all have energy and pattern to spare in 1⅛–1¼oz (32–35.6g) loads in 12 bore guns bored improved cylinder and half choke. No real problems here. It is at flight on the marshes and elsewhere, frequently at the limit of effective shooting (and beyond!) that geese can present such difficult problems - both of lethal loads and of marksmanship. The latter is often the main limiting factor to successful shooting. Good sportsmen will recognise their own limitations here and refrain from shooting beyond their capacity to

Goose loads – patterns at 50 yards (pellets in a 30-inch circle, 12 bore)

Choke	No. 3 shot			No. 1 shot		
	1¼oz (175 pellets)	1½oz (210 pellets)	1⅝oz (228 pellets)	1¼oz (125 pellets)	1½oz (150 pellets)	1⅝oz (163 pellets)
Half choke (40%)	70	84	91	50	60	65
Full choke (50%)	88	105	113	62	85	81

kill – the bane of our 'wildest' sport. The smallest shot size to sustain the necessary penetration at 50 yards (45.7m) is No. 3 (3.3mm), with No. 1 (3.6mm) as the choice of those with faith in its greater penetrative power. Well-choked barrels are an obvious requirement.

Shooters who prefer plenty of pattern will clearly opt for the dense No. 3 loads which will maximise the chance of hits in the vulnerable head and neck area. Those who have more faith in the power of No. 1 shot to penetrate through the toughest part of the quarry should go for the two 'magnum' loads and plenty of choke. Choice here may depend as much on faith as logic!

Goose flighting presents the 'big bore' buffs with an opportunity to exercise their huge 10 and 8 bore guns. Firing anything from 2–3oz (57–85g) of No. 1 or No. 3 shot, kills, on paper, at 60 yards (55 metres) or more can be shown to be feasible. It is often difficult to obtain the necessary experience in the field that such specialised shooting requires. Shooters should therefore again be aware that their skill, or lack of it, rather than ballistic factors can be the main element limiting success in this demanding sport.

CONCLUSIONS

For successful game shooting the evidence points conclusively to the use of standard game cartridges in 12 bore or small-bore guns with a minimum of choke. True cylinder, improved cylinder and possibly half choke

A little more choke and hard-hitting loads are advisable for walked-up shooting.

borings, combined with small shot (No. 6–7) will print optimum lethal patterns from these lightly choked guns. Similar guns loaded with the harder–hitting 1⅛oz (32g) or 1³⁄₁₆oz (34g) loads can be used for really high birds, walking-up, rough shooting and inland fowling. Here, too, modern 20 bore cartridges can prove remarkably effective.

Tight chokes are a distinct handicap to game shooting. Their use, combined with appropriate shot charges, should be restricted to wildfowling at long range.

Standard game cartridges and fairly open chokes are fine for most driven game shooting.

4 Basic Shooting Techniques

It must be said at the outset that there is no definitive technique to good shooting. I am sure that I am far from alone in observing the countless different ways in which people shoot. Many different methods to differing effect, but all doing basically the same thing - raising a gun to the shoulder and pulling a trigger to bring off a successful shot.

Most of those very good good shots have one thing in common, even if their styles are different – they all seem to have time, and their shooting is so effortless. In any sport there are naturals. With practice, the naturals excel, the good become very good and the average can improve beyond their wildest dreams. But the good, and especially the average, not only need to practice, they need to do it properly. The act of simply loosing off lots of cartridges teaches very little other than the simple fact that cartridges can only be used once and their frequent replacement can prove expensive. I have never been a golfer but I read an interesting piece about Lee Trevino (whom even I had heard of). Apparently he was a talented young amateur in Texas when spotted by a potential sponsor who asked him if, with practice, he could win the US Open. He replied that he could. They gave him the sponsorship, he practised and five years later he entered the US Open and duly won it! But even with his talent, it took five years of daily practice.

Those players in most sports who have been able to look after themselves physically can subsequently enjoy higher standards at the end of their careers than they were ever to achieve when at their physical peak. This is simply down to the harnessing of years of experience. And in some cases, such as soccer, this might be in sports where, under most circumstances, fitness would be considered to be everything. Practice and experience are the hallmark of good shots. They shoot skilfully and safely. They shoot with confidence and care. There are those who never shoot from the end of one season to the start of the other and perform faultlessly, but these are few and far between. For the majority there is no substitute for practice. Why should shooting be different from any other sport?

A trip to a local shooting school should set the ball rolling. The likes of Apsley Shooting Grounds are booked solidly from midsummer onwards for pre-season grouse practice. Pheasant practice follows on. Whether it's the local shooting school or clay club, no amount

A visit to a good shooting school will be time and money well spent.

43

of practice can do any harm – unless it is done without any thought or attention to the finer points of good shooting.

WHAT IS GOOD SHOOTING?

Shooting is basically an enjoyable pastime, an outlet and release from everyday life. To get the most out of your shooting you need to put plenty into it – enjoy it, but also take it seriously. Do it well. Shooting well, appreciating your company and environment and respecting your quarry – these are all part and parcel of good shooting. Brilliance is nice, but it's not exactly a common commodity. Almost anyone can shoot competently just as easily as they can be a safe shot. A little application can take you an awful long way.

The Ingredients

The ingredients of good shooting are relatively simple – you take a gun that fits, a stance that's right, a mount that's consistent, a nice smooth swing, and you're there! So, if it's so easy, you ask, how come that more people are not better shots? The answer quite simply is that few bother to take the trouble of mastering the basics. And in the excitement of the moment all of the theory so very often goes straight out of the window. With enough practice, it stays. So let's look at what is needed.

GUNFIT

There can be no underestimating the importance of gunfit. There is no rear sight on a shotgun, the gun being placed at a given point in your shoulder which will align your eyes along the length of the barrel towards the target. If the stock is too short, too long, too high or low, this procedure will be made that much more difficult.

It should, however, be remembered that

There can be no underestimating the importance of gunfit.

during a season you will most likely shoot in every conceivable sort of weather condition, from the warm summer days of grouse moors and duck flights, to cool late November and the bitter cold of January. So, there will be a wide range of garments worn. From early September with a quilted jacket to January layers of sweaters, lining and waxproof, there is quite a difference. The extra thickness worn on those cold days could amount to a stock extension of half an inch (1·25cm) or more. That's another point worth remembering – wear thermal underwear rather than extra layers of clothes.

But back to the gun. Bearing all of this in mind, you need an approximate fit according to the clothing which you expect to be wearing for most of the season.

What is a Perfect Fit?

A perfect fit is achieved when a gun can be mounted time after time (almost sub-consciously) in the same spot, giving its owner the same sight picture on each occasion. He will be seeing just a little of the barrels, so that when he pulls the trigger he will place one third of the shot pattern on or below the target, the remainder on or above. This allows the shooter to keep the target in view up until firing, unless he is taking an overhead driven bird which will be accounted for by the swing-through. It also allows for the fact that because of the fit, the pattern will in any event be slightly ahead of the target.

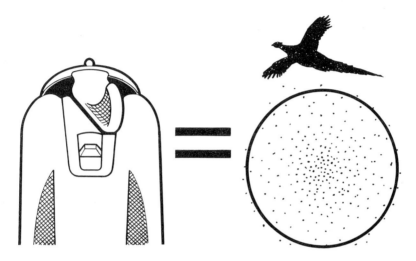

If it is impossible to see any of the rib when the gun is mounted, then the pattern will miss beneath the bird.

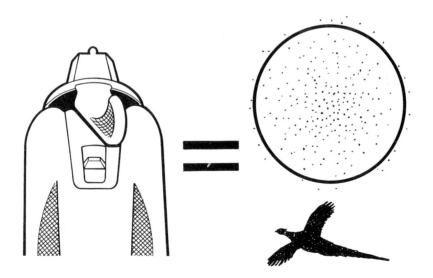

If too much of the rib is visible when mounted, a miss over the top will result.

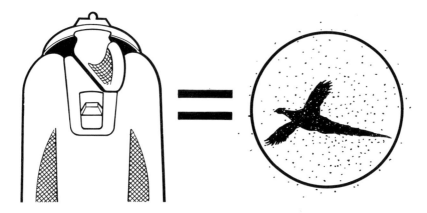

A perfect fit – when just a little of the rib is visible, one-third of the pattern will be placed on or below the target, the other two-thirds on or above.

Stock

The stock is one of the main variable factors on a shotgun – the comb height, the cast and the actual length of the stock itself can make all the difference to your shooting.

The correctly fitted gun will mount smoothly into position and enable its user to look straight down the barrels to the target as naturally as if he were pointing a finger at it.

An average stock length of a side-by-side is approximately 14¾ inches (37·5 centimetres). Due to the single trigger positioning of over-under game guns, their stocks average 14¼ inches (36 centimetres) or 14½ inches (37 centimetres) for a sporting clay model. The gun should simply slide into the shoulder with a minimum of fuss and no movement of the head. Short stocks are a dreadful handicap to good shooting – they result in heavy recoil, which is both uncomfortable and causes 'flinching', and the consequent missing of targets. Key areas apart from stock length are comb height and cast.

Comb Height

Your stock length will be related to the comb itself by the fact that when mounted your cheek will be approximately 1½ inches (3·8 centimetres) from the comb, while the comb height will be a similar measurement. The comb height is the distance between an imaginary continuation line from the rib and the point of the comb of the stock. This and the drop at heel are obviously the crucial areas on any gun. If the stock is too high (with minimal drop at the comb and heel) then the shooter will see a lot of the rib when he takes his shot and he will place the pattern above the bird. Average measurements are 1½ and 2½ inches (3·8 and 6·4 centimetres). A gun on which just a little of the rib can be seen will help lead the eye on to the target.

If the stock is too low, the shooter will see nothing of the barrel rib and will shoot too low (or almost anywhere!). The ideal is where one-third of the pattern is on and below the target and two-thirds on and above. Most well-made modern guns should equate approximately to this, but there are a number which show a substantial difference with the drop at heel.

You should also take into account that we are all made differently and what is right for a slender five-footer is unlikely to be suitable for a Rambo look-alike. So when someone looks at a gun and says the stock is too low, in effect he means that the stock is too low for him. It might be perfect for the owner.

The stock of a gun should be mounted well into the cheek. Do not move the head to the gun, but the gun to the head.

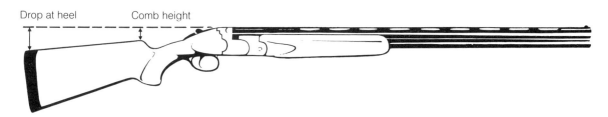

Drop at heel   Comb height

Comb height.

There has been something of a recent vogue for raising stocks on all guns – in some cases regardless of the physique of the owners. Without wishing to be cynical, such a gun will subsequently perform extremely well on straight-driven birds where the fact that it is shooting excessively above the target will automatically give the required lead. But such a gun will come seriously unstuck on birds of any flight that is other than straight-driven. It will shoot over the top of almost everything – with the exception of springing teal.

Conversely, a gun which will shoot on and above its point of aim on a one-third/two-thirds basis enables the bird to be kept in the sight picture at virtually all times and gives the shooter a proper chance of assessing the correct point at which to take his shot.

47

Cast

This is the 'bend' on a stock of maybe only half an inch (1·25 cm) which allows the barrels to align with the eye. This does not vary too much but obviously can be altered to meet the needs of a thin or chubby face, or those with a master eye problem.

The cast enables the barrels to be presented gun to the master eye – which will be right for right-handers, left for left-handers. But a not uncommon problem arises when one eye is not totally dominant. The expert gunfitter or coach will make a point of finding this out at a very early stage. He will check that the gun is empty, give it to its owner and ask him to close it and mount it normally with both eyes open, aiming at the fitter's finger, which will be positioned immediately below the shooter's eye. The chap mounting the gun will then be asked to close his left eye while the gun is still in position. If the picture he sees is the gun pointing at the fitter's finger then all is fine.

By far the most common problem is an only partially dominant right master eye which results in pull to the left. If in such instances the shooter does as he has so often been told, and attempts to shoot with both eyes open, he will probably see up the sides of the barrels (he will certainly do this with an over-under – the broader sighting plane of a side-by-side is an advantage here).

So what is the solution? Quite simply, close one eye. As the target comes into view, keep both eyes open for all-round vision, but as you mount and shoot close or squint one eye in order to concentrate on the target. This should automatically improve your success rate (providing you are doing everything else correctly!). Another big help could come from some extra cant, so presenting the barrel rib to a point suited to your 'balance' of vision.

The real problem occurs when someone who is normally right-handed suddenly discovers that he has a totally dominant left master eye (and of course, vice versa). The shooter is presented with a straight choice – using cross-over stock or shoot from the opposite shoulder. Ask most experienced coaches which is the better solution and they will tell you nine times out of ten to switch shoulders, that is, a right-handed shot should become left-handed. Amazingly enough this switch is not nearly so difficult as it sounds. It might be awkward at first but within a relatively short space of time pupils get the hang of it. In fact, I have come across one or two shots who, after shooting quite ineffectively with their right hands, switched to the other shoulder and saw an improvement almost immediately.

The cross-over stock presents the rib of the barrels to a right-handers left eye. This involves expensive alterations to a gun, which takes on an awkward shape, and offers no better success rate than simply switching shoulders.

Ribs

The rib on a gun is a matter of purely personal taste. The standard side-by-side has a conventional concave rib, while an over-under game gun has a narrow 'game' rib.

Side-by-sides are also found with raised, file-cut ribs and also the Churchill tapered rib. Basically, they all do the same job and while some may have a preference for one or the other, the normal concave rib is as good as anything.

The over-under game gun has a narrower rib than a competition gun. The gun is lighter overall. But there are many who now shoot conventional sporting clay guns for game – and if a shooter has got used to a broad rib then this is what he will probably shoot better with. Again, it comes down to having a familiar sight picture.

Weight

Game guns are now generally reckoned to be pretty light. 'A nice light gun' is a phrase that is often heard. But the value of such a gun is debatable. A gun needs to be light enough not to be a burden on a long day in the field, and so that it can be mounted and shot quickly as and when the occasion arises. Very often you get no warning and chances have to be taken quickly. But it also needs to be heavy enough to withstand recoil and also to help maintain a smooth swing.

It's a question of finding the right compromise. I personally have a weak shoulder and easily feel recoil, so a very light side-by-side is hard work. Similarly, with a 1⅛oz (32g) load, a light over-under can give a sharp kick. One mount in the wrong place and you know about it.

As a yardstick I would prefer a side-by-side in excess of 6½lb (2.8kg) with 1oz (28g) cartridges, and an over-under of between 7lb and 7½lb (3.2 and 3.4kg). I have even enjoyed some excellent days at pheasant with an 8lb (3.6kg) gun. The extra weight doesn't matter so much at driven game where the gun does not have to be carried for any duration. It has caused a few raised eyebrows, but the weight definitely helps my shooting as well as absorbing virtually all of the recoil. Indeed for those very high West Country pheasants a heavy 12 bore will be best to handle the bigger cartridges needed. I must stress that this is a purely personal thing and that for most people who opt for over-unders, a 6¾lb (3kg), the absolute minimum, to 7½lb (3.4kg) would be favourite.

I enjoy 1oz (28g) cartridges, but over-unders can take heavier loads without passing on the side-effects. I also like using a 20 bore over-under which seems to combine the best of several worlds – it is light, but not excessively so in proportion to its dimensions. Because of the smaller loads (23–26g) it doesn't kick, it is quick to handle, and by virtue of the barrel configuration it has pointability. It also offers the added bonus of nice clean kills.

Triggers

Double trigger or single? It makes little difference. The straight hand stock of a side-by-side is arguably better with a double trigger, while the pistol grip of the over-under benefits from single. Switching from one to the other can be a problem. 'Why didn't you shoot at the second bird?' is often the gist of the question that follows any unsuccessful attempt at pulling twice on the front trigger of a side-by-side – or pulling thin air on an over-under!

'Trigger pull' is the amount of resistance on squeezing a trigger and should be in the order of 3½–4lb (1.6–1.8kg) on the first barrel and 4–4½lb (1.8–2kg) on the second. It can be risky having trigger pulls that are excessively light – if caught by gloves, clothing or freezing cold hands, a gun could be accidentally fired. On the other hand, trigger pulls that are too stiff are a fairly common problem, and result in pulling the gun off the line of the shot, so have them checked.

Barrels

The standard game gun has for some years enjoyed barrels of 27 or 28 inches (68.6 to 71cm). Again, this is a length which has evolved as being the best all-rounder.

Robert Churchill was a great salesman for his own guns and advocated not only a shooting technique of the 'never fail' variety but also a special gun to go with it – the 25-inch (63.5-centimetre) barrel. The short barrels were mustard on fast low birds, but time has since proved that on other types of bird they can be difficult to shoot with any consistency, although there are still many who swear by them.

Prior to the breech-loading shotgun, much longer barrels were the norm. But 32-inches (81-centimetres) was scaled down to 30-inches (75-centimetres) breech-loader, and then the 28 and 27-inches (71 and 68.5-centimetres) followed. But it has to be noted that many great shots used a 30-inch where they found that the extra barrel length was an aid to a smooth swing and tracking a target.

This was especially true on very high birds. And the long barrel is in many cases the first choice for the wildfowler, who very often has little other than 'high' birds at which to shoot.

The decision is yours. Certainly 27–28 inches (68·5–71 centimetres) is the best all-round length, but it might be worth trying a 30-inch at some point.

TECHNIQUE

While there is no definitive technique to good shooting, in that there is no *one* way which is the best, all good shots have much in common. Most of all, they make it look easy – and they also seem to have so much time.

Here lies the secret. With good technique, shooting immediately becomes easier, and there is always more time than you think. In all forms of game shooting there is always a tendency to rush. Sight of the bird immediately sets the adrenalin flowing and panic of varying severity can follow shortly afterwards, which in turn prompts a hasty and often wayward shot to be taken.

The man with a good technique will keep his cool, then wait until what he feels is the ideal point at which to shoot before pulling the triggers. You must have seen him in action – he looks 'gifted', an absolute natural blessed with a rare sharpness of eye and a talent which you feel you could never possibly share.

This is mostly untrue. He may be talented, he may have a good eye, but what holds the key to his success more than anything is his ability to shoot properly – to apply concentrated effort with each and every shot, to think out where he should take his shot, keep his cool and apply the correct technique and footwork.

What is Good Technique?

With almost anything in life, if your ground-work is good, everything else will follow. For any form of game shooting the one single factor that must be borne in mind is that to kill a moving target it is necessary to place the shot pattern where the target will be, rather than where it has been. Forward allowance is the essence. It is a simple fact that if a shot is fired 'at' a bird, by the time the thought process has gone into action and pellets have arrived on the line of the bird, it will probably have moved another two or three yards. This is obvious, but as the majority of misses are 'behind', the importance of forward allowance cannot be overstated.

What is needed is a technique which will enable us to judge consistently and accurately the necessary amount of 'lead' or forward allowance, so that when we pull the trigger we know that the shot pattern will have been thrown in the correct direction, that is, the necessary distance in front of the bird to bring off a clean kill.

Though each has its variants, there are two popular methods used in game shooting:

1. To mount and shoot in one flowing motion.
2. To track a target to a given point, then swing through and either fire on the swing or at a calculated distance.

There is also another method, sustained lead, where the gun is mounted at a predetermined distance in front of the target. This is the hardest to master and, quite understandably, is not so common.

The first is the most instinctive style and many feel that this is the most natural and most stylish way to shoot. Some even claim that in doing this they merely shoot 'at' the target in order to hit it, never having to consider forward allowance as the act of mounting the gun will take care of it. I dare say that this is true of fast, low grouse where the birds are shot in front, and modest pheasant, or even quick pheasants that flip across woodland rides, but I personally would prefer to opt for a little deliberation on any bird that comes within the 'high' category, be it pheasant, pigeon, duck or goose.

In any event, what is important to any successful form of shooting is stance and gun mounting. It is impossible to shoot well if the gun is not mounted properly.

Footwork

The advice on footwork for the driven game-bird applies to all species. For most shooting it is vital to stand with your weight on your front (left) foot (right for left-handers). You need a nice easy stance with your feet about nine inches (23 centimetres) apart (I have heard it said that you should stand relaxed as though you were holding a pint, and this would seem to sum it up pretty well). As the bird approaches, the weight can be transferred on to the front foot which will be pointing in the approximate direction of the bird. If it isn't, then a little adjustment is called for.

This is so often one of the key differences between hitting and missing. The eyes and mind will be so intent on the advancing quarry that all thoughts of just about everything else are lost. Assess which direction you expect the bird to take, think about where you intend to take your shot and adjust your feet accordingly. On driven birds there is

Right – by simply moving round to take the shot, the gun has stacked the odds in his favour.

Wrong – the gun has followed the bird without any consideration for footwork. A missed shot is almost inevitable.

almost always time. I'll admit that on duck and geese it can be somewhat more difficult, and sometimes with decoyed pigeon it might be impossible – but every attempt must be made to try to get the body into a position where it is facing the bird. If not, a twist will result in either a dropped shoulder or in the gun stock moving away from the face (often both) and an inevitable miss. Certainly the all-important ingredient of mounting the gun properly will be almost impossible.

Gun Mounting

If you expect to shoot well, you have to mount your gun properly each and every time. Once the fit of the gun is correct, the next objective is to practise until the stock

Mounting the gun – don't leave your thumb near the safety catch unless you want a split nail.

slots home into your shoulder in the same place time after time, so that it becomes a subconscious movement. There should be no movement of the head – the gun will lock neatly into a position where the eyes are looking straight down the barrel.

The best time to mount varies, but the biggest mistake is to mount too early. Instead, as you see a bird come into view, simply watch its approach over the end of the muzzles. Lock your eyes on to it, moving the muzzles up as it approaches. You can always use this period as valuable thinking time, not only assessing its flight but also the where-abouts of other guns – is the bird definitely yours and will it be safe to shoot at it?

When the bird gets close, mount the barrels on to it and follow it briefly before swinging through and pulling the trigger. By following it you will have decided the necessary amount of forward allowance. It is always better to imagine missing the bird in front rather than anywhere else. Mounting the gun on the bird's head rather than its tail feathers will give you that important extra lead necessary to pull off the shot. Modest pheasants can be shot at an angle of around 10 o'clock, while taller birds are better left to 11 o'clock.

If you miss with your first barrel, push on through and there is a very good chance that you will hit with your second. The reason that so many birds are second barrel shots is simply that a kind of hypnosis creeps over the shooter on the bird's approach. He has it in view perhaps for quite a long time. He may have mounted too early, and either poked at the bird or simply neglected to have any follow-through on his shot. This miss prompts him to swing for a second shot which is invariably taken in haste while the gun is in full arc. As a result, the shot pattern is thrown in front of the bird and a kill achieved. Very often spectacular birds are taken in this fashion. There is obviously a lesson to be learned from this.

I know a number of guns who, when seeing a bird coming in their direction, will

When to mount – the feet could maybe be a little closer, but quite a good stance here. Notice how the eyes are looking over the muzzles at the advancing bird.

Still locked on the bird, the gun has been mounted on to it.

The shot is taken and the barrels are still swinging. There is room and time for a second shot.

almost pretend not to see it for a long period, then mount the gun and fire at the very last opportunity. Indeed I have done it myself, often with some success. I do not recommend such a practice as good shooting, but it is indeed an option to be considered as an anti-dote to the 'hypnosis' effect.

While I have been talking mainly about driven shots, the same principles apply for most targets. Apart from some practice at clays, one of the best ways of getting used to gun handling is pigeon shooting. A day in a busy hide (or under a flight line) will see every conceivable kind of shot taken, from driven, to going away, crossing, rising and dropping.

The same basics are relevant on all targets. Watch the bird carefully over the end of the barrels, picking up its line. Mount the gun on the target and at the correct point (where you consider it is at its easiest) move through and shoot. The amount of forward allowance will vary in all instances. But if the gun is mounted properly and the quarry watched carefully, instinct and gun swing will give you the necessary lead. Always remember to keep the barrels moving when pulling the trigger. Just as more birds are missed behind than any-where, very often the reason for such a miss is that the gun has stopped on the squeezing of the trigger. This is one of the hardest parts of shooting, but you will eventually crack it if you continually remind yourself not to 'stop' the gun.

There are times, on particularly long crossers or high birds, when caution must be thrown to the wind and the amount of forward allow-ance will be totally exaggerated. But it must be remembered in such circumstances that there is always a shot string – if you don't catch the bird with the front of the string, you may very well get it with the back. Don't miss behind.

The same principles apply for crossing targets as for driven game – don't mount the gun too early. Watch where the bird is coming from, wait until a point where it is almost at a right angle to you, then mount on the target and move with it before swinging in front and taking your shot.

The overhead shot from behind is often encountered on a pigeon roost shoot or when duck flighting. This time keep the barrels well up in the air, eyes back, and when the bird appears, lock the gun into your shoulder, pick up the bird on your barrels, then move beneath it and shoot.

A shot going away is one quarry for which no clay pigeon can provide a real substitute. For instance, on the second shot at a pheasant which has gone behind the guns, it will almost certainly be dropping in its flight as well as angling. Most shots are missed over the top. Similarly, grouse follow the contours of the land. Duck are rather more predictable, but pigeon can do anything!

Having said that, all of the usual principles apply. However, any shot on this type of target has to be more deliberate. A swift swing into the shoulder and pull of the trigger is really 'hope' shooting. Instead it is better to mount on to the bird and measure it out before deliberately taking your shot, often a little to the side and slightly underneath.

Experience

Good shooting is a combination of instinct and experience. Once the basics have been mastered, the gunfit is good, the stance is correct and the mounting is 100 per cent consistent, then you really are in business.

The more you do, the better you get. Forget preconceptions that clay pigeons are no practice for game shooting. Clays may slow down as they retreat from the trap, but in some cases nowadays this is just as well. Many sporting layouts provide a wide variety of targets that instil in the pupil the need for good mounting and approach work. Once mastered, these skills are seldom forgotten.

If you have a good instructor at your local shooting ground, all the better. Have a couple of lessons, remember your instruction and apply it every time you shoot. The more familiar you are with gun handling the more pleasurable the day's sport will become. The first and foremost requisite for good shooting is being safe. It is vital above all else to be familiar with a gun and gun handling. As with ability, the more you shoot the safer you become – but never take the gun for granted.

5   Pheasant

It's the first drive of the day. Well into November, there's a distinct chill in the air, the leaves are thinning out and drift like giant, rusty snowflakes to the ground with each hesitant breath of what is a fairly soft breeze. The mackerel sky promises a little weak sunshine. The forecast should hold good and the rain is likely to spare us. I am standing in rich, brown sticky plough, about forty yards back from a block of wood which is up the slope in front of me. The peg's plastic number three, wedged in a slit at its top, is printed in bright red letters and also advertises a local game feed company.

I have no dog at my side and look at the next gun to my left where a slender black Lab is being fussed by its owner after retrieving a woodpigeon which flew out of the wood before we had barely taken our guns from our slips. I was inwardly rather envious as I saw it fall from a considerable height in response to an elegant first barrel shot.

All is now quiet as I check and recheck cartridges, the barrels and safety-catch. Will I get a shot? I know exactly how I will take it – or do I? The bird or birds could come from a number of angles. If it's the first one of the day I will be the centre of attention for the entire line of guns, not to mention the picker-up who is stood behind me to my right. 'Just keep cool,' I tell myself.

Looking further back over the picker-up's shoulder, I see another wood which the birds will almost certainly head for. Glancing beyond the guns, I see fields of sugar beet. A tractor is noisily making its way round one of them, a huge green and yellow implement in its wake is spitting leaves and debris in the air. And further on, about a mile and a half away, is the village church. The village itself is quite suddenly bathed in light as the sun sends a shaft piercing through the clouds.

My reverie is interrupted by the screech of a jay. I turn to see it flick up in the trees, veer towards the guns then head back into the wood further down the line. I can now hear the tap-tapping of the beaters. The smell of cigarette smoke drifts across from peg two, and is surprisingly pleasant, evoking memories, no doubt, of other times and other places.

Two simultaneous shots are fired by one of the walking guns. A bird has broken back over the beaters – I wonder if he got it.

'Kok-kok'. A pheasant is in the wood in front of me. There is a whirr of wings and it clatters up into the branches of a big old oak, rapidly climbing into the sky and out into the open. It's coming towards me. My pulse races, I slide the safety forward, raising my barrels, then it swings and banks over in the direction of peg four. I watch as he lifts his gun and just as its stock hits his shoulder, I catch a movement out of the corner of my eye. This time it's definitely mine.

'Wait, wait,' I tell myself. 'Here it comes.' Over the muzzles, into the shoulder, 'it's a cock,' swing in front, and 'yes!'. A silent shriek of delight and the day has started . . .

The dear old pheasant, the most popular of all gamebirds. There's the thrill of grouse in the heather, the excitement of partridges bursting over hedgerows, but for most of us game shooting means pheasant shooting.

The only ground to which the pheasant really takes exception is rocky upland. But as long as there is a mixture of woods, hedgerows and arable land, you will usually find a pheasant (and as long as there is some food at hand, they also show a liking for rough marshland).

The pheasant is not a natural flier. His first choice is always to run. But when he needs to, those big powerful breast muscles will enable him to thrust into the air with great force. Properly presented with guns positioned at a point where they will be beneath the bird at the peak of both its thrust and height, there will be few shots more testing than a tall, curling pheasant.

Contours of land can be used to good advantage here. For a pheasant will rarely fly higher than 35 yards, invariably much less if at all possible. Indeed it is surprising how low many birds are actually shot. So, by presenting birds from either woods or cover crops adjacent to valleys, a reasonably testing shot can easily become a very difficult one indeed. This is certainly applicable to reared birds, which in fact account for the bulk of those which are shot. In excess of 20 million (pheasants and partridges) are released each year. Interestingly, there are a certain number of shoots around the country which still hold a decent stock of wild birds. These tend to be smaller and an altogether sharper proposition. They will climb both faster and higher, or will alternatively find a gap through which to make their exit from the shooting field – much to the annoyance of shoot organisers!

SPORTING HISTORY

So where did the pheasant come from? The brightly coloured cock is a magnificent creature which lends itself so well to snowy Christmas card scenes. His 'loud' appearance is a real give-away that he is not a native of the British Isles. Unlike the distinctly restrained colours of the English partridge, the gaudy cock pheasant is clearly a Continental cousin.

In fact he has now been resident in the British Isles for almost 2,000 years. The first birds were thought to have arrived with the Romans who, keen on their food, were very fond of the pheasant as a bird for the table. The birds were kept very much as farmyard fowl, and certainly not for any sporting uses. These birds were mostly of the Phasis region of the Caucasus, now part of the USSR. No one knows for sure what happened to this original stock – presumably a certain amount became feral, but the real source of today's longtails almost certainly stems back to the Norman period, starting in around 1100. The distinctive birds with white neck rings were introduced much later, at the end of the eighteenth century, and owe their origins to China.

Since that time there has been much inter-breeding and other newcomers, including the bigger Japanese birds and the Mongolian. In many respects all have become known as simply 'pheasant', the one exception being the very dark green bird which is still referred to as Melanistic (this one is of Japanese origin).

The variations can be so wide that it is possible to see a cock that looks virtually identical to a hen. White hybrids are not uncommon – shoot owners like to see one about their shoot and do not look kindly upon guns who disobey instructions not to fire at them.

The great days of pheasant shooting were at the turn of the century, when huge bags were accounted for. This followed the introduction of the breech-loading shotgun which changed the course of the sport in no uncertain manner. It was now possible to shoot vast numbers. And the nature of the landscape, with its perfect mix of woodland and arable, meant that, with vermin control, there would be a big supply of game to be harvested. Stocks were supplemented by large rearing programmes and teams of keepers.

This situation remained unchanged through to the 1950s, although the exclusivity of driven sport was by now substantially eroded. As money spread through the classes (which, in turn, were also being eroded) shooting became available to more people.

Unfortunately there was now taking place a major change in our landscape which saw the felling of large tracts of woodland. England

These are not two hens. The bird on the right is a cock – look at its tail feathers.

needed the wood, but farmers did not need small areas of woodland. Financially they were non-starters, and it made much more sense to clear these parcels of land to make way for other types of cultivation.

Slowly but surely, along with small woods, went hedgerows and ditches (miles and miles of both disappeared from sight). Fields became ever bigger and underground drainage presented even more land to be engulfed by the cereals epidemic. Added to which, while much of Britain's industry was paying lip service to efficiency, farming was setting all the examples. A quiet revolution was taking place around us and the final crowning

glory which was to prove the death knell for much game was the development and dependency on chemicals sprayed on all crops to prevent insect damage and achieve maximum yields.

The farmers should not be criticised – few could foresee that the changes would have had such a dramatic impact on Britain's wildlife.

Research has since shown that a pheasant chick in the first fortnight of hatching will depend almost entirely on insects for its food. If the crops have been sprayed there is precious little to eat. Added to which, if the cover has disappeared, there is nowhere to nest in the first place. And on lowland shoots, where the long, reedy grass of ditchbanks has made way for underground drainage there is also nowhere to nest. Little wonder then that the shoot organiser has become so dependent on the reared bird for his sport.

Much research has been undertaken by the Game Conservancy Trust. Their earlier efforts were mostly channelled in the direction of applying technology and sophistication to rearing systems. Nowadays, with the ever-increasing cost of rearing and releasing, and the likelihood of approximately 40 per cent (maximum) return on birds released, serious consideration is again being given to the wild bird.

Creating a habitat suitable for game is the mood of the moment. Planting small corners of shrubs and woodland, leaving rough areas on shoots, more controlled spraying of crops so as to leave headlands relatively free from noxious chemicals – these are all part and parcel of modern farming and shoot management, plus, of course, the never-ending task of vermin control.

Full marks to the farming fraternity. They have seen what has happened – those farmers who shoot have done far more than most people realise to encourage a return of the wild bird. And, of course, this habitat for game is not only conducive to pheasants and partridges, it offers a haven for all forms of wildlife, whether fauna or flora. 'Show me a land that is keepered, and I'll show you butterflies and songbirds.'

The earnest urban naturalist and self-styled fashionable environmentalist, almost without exception, do precious little for the future of Britain's wildlife. The sporting shot, by necessity, has to put far more in than he can ever take out. He knows his countryside, understands the balance of nature and really is the true environmentalist, in its proper sense.

While there will no doubt always be a liking for big bags, most people nowadays are more concerned with quality shooting – and that applies equally to commercial shoots or syndicated (the syndicate being something of

a backbone of modern-day game shooting). Those commercial shoots who are able to offer quality sport can mostly sell all of their shooting. Others who are simply in the numbers game, putting pheasants over guns, will most likely have to reduce prices to attract customers.

DRIVEN

'Driven' is the most popular form of pheasant shooting, though country-wide there is a lot of pleasure had from walking-up. Driven game shooting is one of the great traditions which is not just simply alive and well, but actually thriving. At the time of writing there is a terrific demand for driven pheasant shooting, and long may it continue. The appeal is understandable. It offers the perfect day out — the company, the surroundings and the excitement of the sport itself.

As the birds are actually driven by a line of beaters from either cover crops or woodland in front of a line of guns, it would seem fair to assume that all of the shots presented would be very similar. Indeed, Fleet Street is fond of reminding the general public (who they obviously assume to be as ignorant as themselves) that such birds are kicked into the air, only to be 'blasted' out of the sky.

But all, as they say, is not what it seems, and this is the appeal of the game shooting. No two birds are alike. There will mostly be between five and eight drives during the day. Some may be similar, but none identical. Typically, a line of eight to ten guns will be positioned in widely varying settings and birds will be driven from entirely different cover.

The correct driving of pheasants is an art all of its own. Seldom do good pheasant drives 'just happen'. Some shoots are lucky in that they have perfect land off which to present their birds. But very often the relevant woodland has been specifically planted for this purpose and, without exception, the same applies to cover crops.

You don't need hills to present good quality birds. A skilled keeper and organiser will know of many ways of giving challenging sport to the guns.

TECHNIQUES

Stance

The birds having been flushed from cover will be heading for the next nearest, apparently safe retreat, mostly behind the guns. It is virtually impossible to stage a good pheasant drive if the birds have nowhere specific to head for. The first relevant point to be borne in mind, then, is 'where will they fly?'

Having gone to your peg, you will immediately have a good look round. You will look in front to the wood or other cover from where they will be flushed, and you will look behind to see where they are likely to be heading. While doing this a prime consideration will be to check whether a picker-up and his dog are standing behind you. Sadly, all too often people get carried away in the heat of the moment and, after missing a bird with their first shot, will turn and shoot as it flies behind them. The subsequent shot may well result in pellets flying around the picker-up.

Check, too, the position of the guns on

either side. Keep in the line and make a mental note of the safe positions at which to shoot as well as the ones where you won't be poaching others' birds.

Taking your gun from your slip, and keeping the muzzles pointing downwards, open it and check the bores are clear. Slip two cartridges into the breech, close the gun, still pointing downwards, and either hold it over your arm or with the stock resting against your thigh and the barrels pointing upwards.

While I appreciate that such instruction is just about as basic as you can get, having a routine is all part and parcel of good shooting. A particular habit of mine is checking that the bores are clear of dirt and other particles. While standing and waiting I will often remove the cartridges to double-check that everything is in order. This has become a habit, and while I am over zealous, I feel it better to be doubly sure than simply trusting to luck.

Holding the gun safely – the muzzles are pointing at the earth. Remember, either heaven or hell!

A good relaxed stance – it wasn't surprising that this was a successful first barrel.

Note how the shoulder has dropped the weight on to a crouched back leg – the gun will not align properly with the eyes and the bird will most likely be missed.

Approach

If the odd pigeon flies out of the wood early on in the drive, be sure that you are allowed to shoot before you let off your gun at one. Some shoots prefer that no cartridges be fired until the first pheasant appears. Strangely enough this period of waiting for the beaters' advance can be one of the most exhilarating experiences. You have no idea of what is about to happen – it is a period of both contemplation and excitement. For once you have time in this hectic world to stand and stare, and it's surprising what can be seen.

Eventually there are noises emanating from the wood. The odd shot rings through the air as a far-off walking gun attempts to prevent the escape of a wily cock. Up front, the wood becomes alive with movement. Jays, tits and blackbirds show themselves. Blackbirds cause many a flinch with their flight, uncannily resembling a game species as they spring out of the wood in front of the guns. You hear the odd 'kok-kok' of a pheasant and you will involuntarily spring to attention. You will stand upright but at ease, and holding your gun so that the barrels are pointing upwards.

You might see guns who start with their muzzles pointing at the earth, and when a pheasant heads in their direction they will mount the gun with an almighty sweep through the air. Apart from making for difficult shooting, this is also a dangerous

Despite a number of pheasants in the air, the gun has kept his cool and waited to pick out his bird at the ideal shooting point.

practice as the gun is clearly going through the line of beaters. Instead, it is better to stand with the gun angled upwards and your gaze fixed over its muzzles. When you anticipate that a bird is getting up in front of you, be at the ready. You will let your weight fall on to your front foot (left, for right-handers), your body facing the direction from which the bird is advancing. You will continue to watch the bird until a point a little after 45 degrees, when, keeping the muzzles on the bird, you will mount on to it, pulling through and shooting at the correct moment.

Shooting in Front

It's nice to see people shooting their birds in front, that is, at a point well before they have reached the gun, but this is a practice best left to lower birds, and even then only when it is completely safe. If a gamebird is flying at any height, the point at which it will be nearest to you, and also the easiest at which to judge its range, will be when it is overhead. If you shoot slightly in front of this, at 11 o'clock for example, then you will have the chance of a second barrel if the first fails to connect. You can try 10 o'clock on a lower bird.

Forward Allowance

If you aim at and shoot at a moving target with a stationary gun, your shot pattern will arrive at where the target has just been. It is a simple fact that in order to connect, you must shoot at the point where the target will be at the time your shot pattern reaches its destination.

In the time it takes to pull a trigger and for a cartridge pattern to reach a pheasant at 30 yards (27·4 metres), that bird will in theory have travelled 5 feet 6 inches (168 centimetres). You don't need to be a mathematician to point out that in order to connect with that pheasant, the man pulling the trigger must make an allowance of the same distance. A 30-yarder is a good bird, though not exceptional, and this example shows how a shooter really has to be

A high pheasant – eyes over muzzles watching the oncoming bird.

Eyes still on the bird, the gun is now in the shoulder and swinging smoothly through.

By watching the bird and establishing a smooth swing, the brain will automatically decide the necessary forward allowance.

on his toes. There are three main variables in this:

1. Is there a good smooth swing on the gun?
2. Does the shooter move the gun to the required distance but stop moving at the time he pulls the trigger?
3. How quickly does the gun swing on mounting?

As a result of one or all of these, the assessment of forward allowance will vary enormously according to the individual. You should not, therefore, listen to recommendations of lead to be given for certain birds. A shooting instructor will be able to assess how you are reading a bird and by watching you take a few shots, will be able to tell you exactly how much lead to give a bird. But ignore the advice of others who have no such expertise. A man with a fast mount and swing will have

Watch the curl and leave it for your neighbour.

a totally different sight picture to a deliberate 'point it out' type of shot. Moreover with game shooting, unlike clay pigeons, birds coming from a given direction can be travelling at different speeds and heights. This is one of the most awkward determining factors in good pheasant shooting. And it's never any use simply swinging in front of a curling pheasant to a given distance without that swing being on the curling flight line of the bird.

Practice really does make perfect when assessing forward allowance. With good style and approach work the 'natural' who plays

cricket, tennis and golf only once every three years and excels at all will similarly be able to come to terms with what is needed. He has the hand-eye-brain co-ordination. But it is not such a problem even for us lesser mortals, providing we too pay proper attention to the approach work. With good stance, consistent mounting and a smooth swing on to the bird and through it, we will enjoy the kind of success rate that gives additional pleasure to the day's sport.

Remembering the Shot String

One the wisest (and nicest) owls I have had the pleasure of knowing was Chris Cradock. What Chris didn't know about guns and shooting wasn't worth knowing, and if he said something which didn't seem 100 per cent technically sound, you knew there must have been a very good reason for him saying it. I'll have to admit that when he once told me that one of the most important considerations on teaching a pupil is shot string, I thought to myself 'what possible difference can a shot string make when it is travelling at 1,100 feet per second? You'll either hit the target or you won't'.

Of course, the real difference that a shot string makes is in the mind of the shooter. You must instil in him that he can safely shoot further in front than he need because he can connect with the tail of the shot string if he has gone too far. But if he isn't far enough ahead, the whole column will miss. This may be theoretically, and practically, true but the real advantage of considering the shot string is giving the shooter the confidence to move far enough in front of the bird to give it the necessary forward allowance. Pheasants are missed in all sorts of places. The shot can fly at any point around a bird, but 99 times out of 100 a missed shot whizzes past the tail feathers.

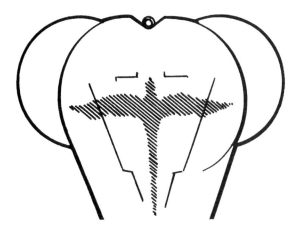

If none of the rib is visible then, in order to shoot at a pheasant on pattern, it is necessary to obscure it totally.

A little of the rib would enable the target to be kept in view as it is reached.

A nice smooth swing through the pheasant – keep the barrels moving.

Stopping the Gun

Perhaps the most common reason for missing is stopping the gun. Having picked up the line of the bird and mounted the gun, all of us at some point or other will swing through to what we feel is the necessary distance and then pull the trigger and halt the swing all in one. The shot will automatically go where the bird has been! Some will try to overcome this lack of gun movement with a flick at the last minute. This can be partially successful – indeed, I must own up to such a ploy myself, and have used it to good effect. But I must also admit that on other occasions it has let me down badly.

There is never any substitute for sticking to the one tried and trusted method of a good smooth swing – and keeping the gun moving after the shot has been fired.

Right and Left

This is the art of bagging two birds with successive shots, not having time to reload and the gun most likely remaining in the shoulder between shots. When the chance presents itself you will have seen the two birds and mentally noted 'these are mine'. The adrenalin will start, but you must endeavour to switch off the supply. Carefully and coolly, calculate which is the better bird to take first. Pheasants are unlikely to fly one behind the other in a line – they mostly divide in front of you.

65

The bird is at an ideal point for taking the shot. Ignore the fact that it may be gliding – it will be travelling every bit as fast as if its wings were beating.

The camera lens makes the birds appear more distant than they actually were. The gun pulled off a right and left by methodically taking one pheasant at a time.

If they are more or less equidistant from the gun, the right-hander will look to take the right-hand, or straighter, bird first, and then the left. The reason for this is that despite following all the correct style and approach work, a late right-handed shot might result in a sharp twist of the body and as the gun swings right, the stock moves away from the face, the shoulder drops and a hit is nigh impossible.

Taken the other way, as the gun swings left, the stock is pushed tight into the face and the mount is locking the gun in position, the eye at all times looking down the barrel.

But perhaps the most important point of all is to shoot only one at once. You can't bag two until you have hit the first one. So, having noted that there are two in front of you and decided which bird you intend going for first, forget about the other one until you have shot and made sure of the first one. Then concentrate solely on the second, going through the motion of putting your barrel on to the bird and then swinging through and shooting. Don't simply poke at the second bird in hope.

Footwork

A good point to remember about shooting a right and left – indeed any bird – is that it doesn't take a second to adjust your body and stance. If you have shot one bird facing a certain direction, and the two birds are not close to one another, it may be better (indeed it very often is better) to pause, adjust your position, and shoot the second bird from a different angle.

I make no apologies for repeating myself – there is usually more time than you think. I know that I have found it hard to believe sometimes, but watch the guys who can really knock them down. They don't get into contorted positions – they take a shot cleanly and simply, perhaps move a little for the second one, and repeat the exercise.

Another option for high birds is to turn sideways, so as to take the pheasant as a crosser.

Head Down

Another major cause for missing is lifting the head off the stock. 'Keep your head down' is great advice which we can always administer to ourselves when shooting. Too often we mount the gun, then briefly lift our eyes just as we shoot. It is something which happens almost subconsciously and requires a mental kick up the backside to keep it under control.

This is a common fault found in snooker and billiards. A player lines up a ball perfectly, but just as he makes the stroke, he lifts his head away from the cue. In cricket the batsman takes his eye off the ball at the last vital minute. Both spell disaster – and it's the same in shooting. Only through luck will you hit a target that you are not looking at properly.

Shooting Behind

There will always be instances where there isn't time to get a second shot off as the bird approaches. Perhaps you pricked it – or maybe you feel that if you swing round you will be in a perfect position to drop it. Were there any pickers-up behind you? How far can you see? Never shoot into cover – someone may have moved into a bramble while you were scanning forwards for an oncoming bird.

If you are clear to shoot behind, the first rule is always to turn with your barrels out of the shoulder and muzzles pointing skywards. Remember, you are carrying a loaded gun that is built to kill. Turn round completely, don't just twist your body. Having turned, look carefully at the bird, which may well be planing down to land. Again, pick up its line, and I would suggest a little deliberation. I don't mean poking at the bird, but measuring it out so that your line will most likely go in front (but will appear to be pulling the gun to its side) and maybe slightly underneath, to allow for its drop. A quickly mounted shot will hit it cleanly up the backside – or miss over the top.

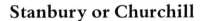

More birds are missed behind than anywhere else – don't stop the gun swing when you pull the trigger.

The Churchill style of shooting high pheasants with the weight on the back foot.

Stanbury or Churchill

You will note that I have mentioned, in all instances, that the driven bird is taken off the front foot. This is very much in the style of Percy Stanbury, the famous instructor who for many, many years taught at West London Shooting School. Robert Churchill had different ideas on footwork and would recommend taking high birds off the back foot.

His reasoning was that with the arching of the back for a high bird, a front-foot shot would strain to take his second barrel, while the back-footed counterpart, with his different back stance, was more free to manoeuvre. Certainly guns of a bigger build (particularly girth!) may well find it easier to shoot high birds off the back foot.

Both stances are good. It is a matter of what suits the individual. Interestingly, I feel that the front foot method lends itself rather well to Churchill's 'mount and pull the trigger' style of shooting. He encouraged the shooter to rely on a more confident, instinctive style of shooting. Good for 'natural' shots and for attacking fast, low birds – but not perhaps for the average shot, particularly the chap who varies his sport rather than concentrating solely on driven.

Back foot shooting, incidentally, is not to be confused with a 'legs astride' approach, where the shooter stands as if ready for combat!

Reloading

This can always be a tricky one. The first object, of course, is to do it safely. Barrels pointing to the ground, a quick look down the barrels as you drop two more in, close and then lift the muzzles to the air (but not through the line). The big problem area arises when you have shot a first barrel bird, and you decide to reload. Just as you open the gun, another bird appears. There is no hard and fast solution to this one – other than to apply a good portion of common sense.

Woodland Rides

There will be times when you find that your peg is at the back of a very narrow woodland

There is sometimes little time to see a bird in woodland rides and this gun has quickly dropped his weight on his 'wrong' foot, but his stance is otherwise very sound. He pulled off a fairly smart shot.

ride. Thoughts of picking out your bird and waiting to mount have to be concentrated into very tight pockets of fractions of seconds. In essence the same principles apply. But here more than ever, the man who can mount a gun properly and consistently will win hands down.

Again, one key point to remember is that most pheasants follow a line to a 'home' wood or cover. You can face the expected direction of flight, and listen carefully. If you suspect any deviation, adjust your position accordingly and have your muzzles well in the air, ready to mount on to the bird as soon as you see it. You will then have an opportunity to get on to it and quickly track it for shooting. It's surprising what you can cram into a couple of seconds! Don't worry here about rights and lefts. Think only of one at a time if you get a second shot in, all well and good.

CONDUCT

Marking Birds

If you have picker-up behind you, do your host a favour and get on with the shooting. The dog handler will look after any birds you may have shot. But if there are no dogs at hand, make sure that you mark any birds which you feel you may have pricked. A wounded pheasant can travel a surprisingly long way. He may well be dead when he lands, or perhaps lying up in a rabbit hole or tree root. Your host, in this situation, will want this bird in the bag. Watch it land, mentally mark the point then resume the shooting.

Poaching Birds

The one man who is always unpopular is the clever dick who starts shooting birds which really belong to the gun at the next peg. He claims he never knows he has done it, or pretends that he didn't notice. This is merely

There are times when the host will have asked that you don't shoot hen birds, or that you should be selective on low pheasants. Be sure before you shoot.

greed. The day is not a competition as to who can shoot the most, and if you are in any doubt that a bird is yours, don't raise a gun to it. It's far nicer to be thought of as a courteous shot than a garrulous one.

There will always, of course, be the odd time when you shoot and then realise that the bird was curling in your neighbour's direction. Without any hesitation, raise your hand in apology. He will understand – unless he happens to be the one who normally does the poaching (in which case he will probably get terribly upset about it!).

Unsafe Shots

There's nothing more likely to spoil a day's shooting than standing next to an unsafe gun. It is a terrible experience having to suffer someone who is either very inexperienced, excitable or thoughtless (or even worse, all of these).

Forget about upsetting others' feelings, guns are dangerous weapons and any mistake could be fatal. So, have no hesitation in pointing out the wayward nature of your neighbour's shooting habits. Don't, however, be stroppy about it. He may still be wearing his 'L' plates and totally unaware of the fact that he is swinging through the line (or something equally frightening). Have a quiet word with him. Explain to him the serious nature of what he is doing, that there is no need to mount a gun early (often a problem, and it also puts beaters in danger), and that the birds he should shoot at are those in the air above him.

If you feel that the individual in question is unapproachable and doesn't respond even to a call of 'Oi!', have a discreet word with the shoot host. If you have any doubts at all, you should do this in the first instance. It is, after all, he who invited the offending party. It is his duty to ask him to be more careful.

It has to be said that this is the one disturbing aspect of 'company days', where the host will assemble a team of guns consisting entirely of clients and business acquaintances. Rather than oiling the wheels of industry with golf weekends and trips to Ascot, there are quite a number who take a day on a commercial pheasant shoot. There is nothing wrong with this – in fact, it can be very good for the sport, in as much as each year there are now hundreds of new people who are given a taste of the fascination of pheasant shooting. But it is the duty of all shoot hosts to make sure that all guests are safe and can handle a gun proficiently.

There's nothing worse than dropping a pheasant at someone else's feet.

Gundogs

For many, indeed most people who go shooting, one of the greatest pleasures is seeing their dog work. A nice shot followed by an excellent retrieve will make a man's day. However, not all gundogs are quite as good as their owners tend to think they are. The rose-tinted view of dogs expressed in conversations over a couple of drinks means nothing in the field. And there is nothing more guaranteed to upset everyone present than a dog that is either unable to keep quiet, or insists on chasing everything in sight.

A gamekeeper may have worked long and hard on creating a particular drive. He will have nurtured trees and cleared undergrowth. He will have maintained vigils to catch poachers. He will have reared pheasants through difficult weather conditions. And he will have done everything humanly possible to prevent pheasants from straying and to keep vermin under control.

He will have been out of bed extremely early on the day of the shoot. The beaters will have been organised and briefed and then, when they have 'brought in' the wood (carefully walked an adjacent field and hedgerow

71

Too low – this pheasant may well swing and rise on the wind to present a good sporting shot to a gun at the other end of the line, which in this instance was in an 'L' shape.

to move any game into the wood) they will have patiently gone through the wood itself.

But just as they get to the point where the pheasants will start to flush, they see a dog charging in front of them, scattering game everywhere! (The offending dog probably saw a rabbit and bolted.) Such an animal (and owner) can not only spoil the drive, but the day itself. The keeper quite understandably will be incensed. So if you take a dog, be sure that he will not be an embarrassment.

On the other hand, a well-behaved gun-dog will be welcomed on any shoot. Indeed, it will probably earn its owner a number of invitations. I will not enter into any arguments as to which dog is best. We all have our preferences, and whether it's a Lab or Springer, dog or bitch, is a matter of choice for the owner. To the other guns the main consideration is whether the dog is obedient and capable of fulfilling its duties on the day.

A good gundog is the perfect companion at your peg.

Alcohol

One of the other accompaniments to a day's driven pheasant shooting is alcohol, in one form or another. Again, this is a matter of common sense. On a cold winter's morning, a sloe gin really does go down a treat. And a drop may also take away the tension, enabling you to be a little more relaxed and confident with your shooting.

A couple of drinks in the warmth of lunch-time are especially welcome, but there are also far too many stories of shooting accidents or narrow escapes after extended lunches.

Certainly the shoot lunch is very enjoyable and an integral part of the day. You'll most likely be extremely hungry. Food never tastes better than after a long morning in the fresh air – and the company and stories will be good. However, the entire atmosphere is conducive to having a drink or two too many. I know of one shoot host who after an extensive lunch, stood up at the table and said: 'OK, let's see if we can fit a couple more drives in before the next drink.' It was actually quite funny at the time, but it certainly illustrates a point.

Many more shoots are arranging the shoot meal at the end of the day rather than the middle, merely stopping after four or five drives for a spot of soup and sandwiches. There's a lot to be said for this, particularly on those short winter days when stopping for lunch can cut a large hole in shooting activities.

Hip flasks are fun. There are so many different shoot concoctions, but again, while a sip or two might be OK, be careful not to overdo it. A drop may relax you, but two or three drops will spoil your shooting, will probably make you dangerous, and will get your alcohol level to a point where you will break the law if you drive home. A final thought – in extreme cold, alcohol can be very hazardous to your health.

Tipping

At the end of the day there is mostly a tip for the keeper. Check with your host as to the actual amount, as this tends to vary quite a lot these days. On some shoots you may also be asked to chip in towards the cost of the beaters.

SHOOT ORGANISATION

Bought Days

More and more people are turning to 'bought days' for their sport. While the syndicate is

At the end of the day, it should be remembered that it is your host and gamekeeper who have made it all happen. Some appreciation is always well received.

still popular, there is now an increasing number of agents who are either running shoots or merely letting them on behalf of others. These offer shooting without the year-round commitment which for some is now impossible. Many guns who are in syndicates also like to try a day's sport in another part of the country, so they simply buy a day.

In fact, roving syndicates depending entirely on bought days, are now quite common. The agent can offer a variety of sport. You can choose location, setting and, of course, the anticipated bag. It all sounds too good to be true. Unfortunately, standards vary enormously. While there are many reputable agents offering very good sport and fair value, there are others who know nothing of integrity. So if you are thinking of buying a day, it will be advisable to observe the following guidelines:

1. Use either a well-known agent, or preferably an agent or shoot which has been recommended to you by someone with first-hand experience.
2. Confirm the anticipated bag and the cost.
3. Make it clear that you will not wish to exceed the quoted bag.
4. Check what extras will be involved.
5. Is VAT included?
6. Will drinks and meals be included?

Hidden extras can ruin a day. I know of many guns who have bought their shooting, only to find that virtually everything is charged as extra. Another trick, particularly on larger days, is to achieve the bag before the day's natural conclusion, and then ask the guns if they wish to continue. If so, the additional birds will be charged at a given amount per head. This places the guns in an awkward position. They will most likely have just had an excellent drive and will find it difficult to resist the temptation to continue. Unfortunately there may be a couple of the guns in the team who are not in a position to afford or justify the additional expense, and quite rightly would prefer to end the day's activities at this point. They will not, however, wish to spoil the party so will reluctantly agree to continue. It will prove a costly treat and a salutary experience. Even if the extra birds are at a cheaper rate, the team will end up paying far more for their day out than originally budgeted.

From the point of view of the guy running the shoot, this increased bag is good news. The additional birds have been shot at no extra cost – he will not pay the beaters any more for the extra drive. They have come for the day, and the extra drive is merely part of that day. You should also watch the host who shoots back gun to finish off the pricked birds – he may well account for 30 per cent of the bag.

While I don't want to tar all shoot agents with the same brush, and must stress that the majority are very good, it is important for all concerned to know exactly where they stand before the shooting commences.

One or two syndicates or private farm shoots are now also letting days. These can vary enormously. Very often the people running such shoots have little commercial experience. It is one thing to have invited someone to a shoot purely as a guest, when the bag doesn't meet expectations. No money has changed hands and nothing more is thought of it. But if that shooting has been bought, we are talking about a whole different ball game.

Similarly, if you are a member of a shooting syndicate, be guarded if your shoot captain suggests that a day be sold to offset costs. If the bag varies drastically on your own days, then why should this change when a visiting team of guns arrives on the scene? If, however, your shoot runs like clockwork, the bags are predictable, you feel that the quality is good and that you have a surplus of game, then selling a day can indeed be a good idea. My own feeling, however, is that it is better to leave shoot letting to the people who make it their business. It can get very complicated, not to mention financially awkward!

Starting the Day

On any shoot it is absolutely vital that at the beginning of the day you pay attention to your host when the peg numbers are drawn. You not only need to know your peg number, but also how many pegs you move at the end of each drive. And you will particularly listen to the rules with regard to ground game – and, indeed, any other do's and dont's.

If later on during the day you see someone shooting at a hare, when you have been asked not to, don't follow his example. Keep your day enjoyable by doing as you are told.

Double Guns

On big days (minimum 300), guests may shoot double guns, that is, using two guns, with someone to act as a loader. This is in fact quite a skilled operation, where the gun and his loader will need to operate quickly, slickly and safely in order to shoot well in the face of a *battue* of pheasants. It is here that a perfectly matched pair of guns comes into its own.

Double Banking

Occasionally there are drives on which pheasants tend to channel over two of the pegs. These are very often when birds are flying off a hill towards a 'release pen' wood. If the eight guns were pegged normally in one long straight line, the two guns at either end might get very little shooting, so the drive is rearranged so as to peg perhaps a couple of the guns 30 or 40 yards back from pegs three and four. Again, safety is very important for guns taking these positions.

Bag Size

One of the fascinating aspects of shooting is that no matter where you go, the first question you are asked after your day's sport is, 'How many did you get?'. Yet while getting a decent bag can be a reflection of whether you have had a good day, this in itself tells but part of the story. Driven pheasant shooting falls into a number of bag categories, and it doesn't matter whether the bag is 80 or 280, your pleasure will mostly be dependent on one or two particular shots, the company and actually being there.

A small bag may indicate a lack of birds or it may mean that the shooting was more difficult. In order to achieve big bags there are a number of shoots who will lay on relatively easy shooting. And, of course, with a profusion of game, as the day progresses the shooting becomes more accurate with practice.

The 'luck of the draw' is one of those sayings that lends itself to driven pheasant shooting (indeed, it is thought to have been one of many that owe its source to it). On a day which realises a bag of 120, it is quite possible to have quite a lot of shooting or,

Happiness is . . . a well-taken brace of cock pheasants.

conversely, fire only two or three shots. This is particularly so on a line of ten guns. Work it out this way: ten guns means an average of twelve birds per head (which may well be ample), at one and a half birds per drive per person. But there are inevitably one or two hotspots where a given peg may produce a dozen birds. Three or four drives like that drastically reduce the odds for the other guns. I myself have been on a shoot where, despite a good lunchtime score, I had fired only one cartridge (at a pigeon) during the entire morning. I had half a dozen shots in the afternoon, but my day could so easily have ended in a blank.

The real measure of a day is the pleasure it gives you. And that can mean anything from six birds to 600.

WALKING-UP

The art of walking and stalking pheasants with gun and dog stretches back to the muzzle-loader. Only with the perfection of the breech-loading shotgun did walking-up start to play second fiddle to driven shooting.

Today, walked-up shooting gives pleasure to thousands. Anyone who has been out with a couple of pals, walked a few miles of hedgerows and bagged a pheasant or two with the odd rabbit or hare and half a dozen pigeon will tell you what a marvellous day he has had. There is something entirely natural and very satisfying about walked up shooting. It is perhaps the thought that any game shot is hard earned, or maybe the application of some fieldcraft. Certainly a key ingredient in your success is getting to know the 'right spots' and corners which are likely to be productive. Small spinneys, clumps of brambles and perhaps an overgrown bank of a drainage ditch might all yield a pheasant.

Having walked a couple of miles, on a cold winter Saturday, your dog quite suddenly gets the scent of a pheasant. Before you have any thought about responding a cock

Once you know the likely spots, it is possible to flush birds for one another.

pheasant clambers into the air almost at your feet. It is an exciting moment, and a cartridge fired in haste is one most likely wasted.

While your instincts and reactions will want to be quick, they must also be calculating. If a bird rises close to your feet, you certainly have plenty of opportunity of mounting and shooting when it reaches a half decent range of approaching 20 yards. In such an instance there is a tendency to mount quickly, almost by instinct. You may, however, be wearing quite a lot of clothing, and find that your gunstock catches on your jacket. Consequently, you pull the trigger with the butt nowhere near the correct mounting position. By shooting at close range you will also have very little shot pattern and you will either miss the bird completely or reduce it to pâté.

The 'one man and his dog' approach can be further enhanced by the company of a couple of friends. The three of you can cover a much larger area of ground and with good use of fieldcraft can detect those places which will offer a route of escape for your quarry.

Indeed, even with only a couple of you, it is possible to flush birds for one another. One gun can stand hidden at the end of a likely piece of cover while the other walks through with a dog. The bird may well not be orthodox driven but you will probably be presented with a very good sporting shot (and maybe a really testing long crosser).

The first rule of shooting in these situations is to be especially safe. Remember your safety zones at all times, and ensure that you are not swinging through a line where people are likely to be positioned.

Be at the ready when your dog gets the scent of a bird – but also be careful of the dog.

A gundog is essential for walking-up.

Which Gun?

Your usual game gun should be fine for walking-up, although some may argue that they prefer a little more choke for going-away birds. It must be remembered, however, that modern cartridges with plastic wads throw tight patterns and that quarter choke (and certainly half) should cover most eventualities. The 20 bore over-under is an ideal walking-up gun with its pointability matched with lack of weight.

Gundog

A dog is absolutely vital for walking-up. It improves your shooting by flushing birds that may have otherwise sat tight and also adds to your bag in other ways. You will not wish to hit a bird and go home empty-handed. There is nothing that spoils a day more than the thought of having been unable to locate a wounded bird.

Permission

This is stating the obvious, but don't go on any land unless you are absolutely sure of obtaining permission from its owner. Don't simply accept the word of someone who might not be in a position to give permission.

6 GROUSE

Leaning forward against the damp, stony wall of the butt, the view in front is limited by a sharply rising bank out of which clusters of heather are doing battle with the grass and bracken. But to my right the moor goes sweeping down and I am looking from what seems an almost imperious height towards three adjacent butts, surrounded in a sea of purple. A stream cuts its way through the rock and vegetation at the bottom of the incline. It is filled and gurgling with fresh water. A huge sky is predominantly blue but streaked with extended shreds of whiter than white cloud. A cool wind is a lingering calling card for the snow and icy weather that is but a couple of months away.

All is absolutely silent. Because of the hill in front I cannot even see any birds on their approach. But there is a shot down the hill, and then three or four more. Adjusting my vision I can see a largish pack of grouse splitting either side of the end butt. Dark, bulbous bodies with flashes of white; two or three have curled high and away – others have dropped sharply, to cling close to the heather.

The birds are on the move and the white flags of the flankers are waving frantically. A pack must be about to . . . here they are. Gun in the shoulder. One shot in front. Miss. Turn – the birds are banking away. One to the rear. On to him, through and . . . yes!

HABITAT AND DISTRIBUTION

There is little wonder that the opening day of the grouse shooting season is christened the Glorious Twelfth. It is without doubt the most celebrated day on the game shooting calendar. There is only one other date

(1 September for duck) which is religiously adhered to as an 'off-the-blocks' start. And there is arguably no finer place on earth than in a grouse butt on the Twelfth.

The awesome setting is like no other. Grouse country is as wild as the bird itself. On a moor, the everyday world seems more than a million miles away – it ceases to exist. This really is a world apart, and so is grouse shooting.

Alas, it is also the most expensive form of game shooting. In the cold context of modern day economics, it's all down to supply and demand. Despite vast tracts of moorland habitat in Scotland and the North of England, there are not enough grouse to go round. And, unlike pheasant and partridge, this is a bird which does not lend itself to rearing. In fact, no such thing as a rearing and release programme exists.

The red grouse is a subspecies of the willow grouse and unique to the British Isles. There are other members of the family found in much smaller numbers – the blackcock, ptarmigan and capercaillie.

It would appear that the real problem is not so much rearing as releasing. After feeding the chicks in the rearing pen, the young birds find it impossible to come to terms with the coarse heather once released. All shoots are therefore completely dependent on wild stocks.

The moors themselves cover large areas of land which up until the eighteenth century were mostly wooded. When the forests were cleared, they gave way to heather, grass and bracken – the more heather, the more grouse. And as the grouse is largely dependent on heather for its diet (though it also eats various berries and shoots) this is none too surprising. Like all game, in order to maintain any stock, it is necessary to provide the correct environment. Controlled heather burning in the spring will encourage a continual new growth of heather, thus giving the birds the nourishment needed. Similarly, vermin control is also very important.

But grouse are complex creatures and apart from being prone to two serious diseases, are also subject to inexplicable variations in their stocks. Moor owners have always been used to these ups and downs, but there was a disastrous run of downs in the 1970s which had everyone scratching their head. The expected improvement never came and much research has since been undertaken into the causes.

Clearly, by favouring a moorland habitat (mostly 1,000 to 2,000ft (305 to 610 metres) above sea level), they are much more prone to the vagaries of the weather and a late spring can cause a lot of damage. But on the other hand these are tough little creatures and the weather has been a simple enough explanation. The diseases strongylosis and louping ill both undoubtedly take a considerable toll. Strongylosis is a minute threadworm, and particularly prevalent when moors are carrying large stocks of grouse. Shooting obviously helps in such instances. The older birds (the more prone to the disease) will mostly fly first and consequently are much more likely to be shot, leaving a stock of healthier, younger grouse.

Louping ill virus is mostly passed on to grouse by sheep ticks. This is more of a problem in Scotland than England. But in any event, for one reason or another – weather, disease, environment, vermin – two out of three grouse will die in their first twelve months. But given the right habitat and a good rearing season, the birds will return in good numbers.

After several years of much despondency, many moors showed dramatic increases in stocks in recent times. And while there were some noted moors that continued to flop, the improvements were especially good news for many reasons. Softwood forestry (an absolute haven for vermin) was spreading like a plague on many estates, and consequently robbing prime grouse country in the process. As incomes from grouse shooting continued to plummet, there was an increased likelihood that landowners would look to plantations as a viable alternative.

With a sign of the grouse returning they might think again. With such a huge demand for grouse shooting, it is quite possible to charge sums of up to £120 per brace. This is a welcome return on vast areas of land which, apart from sheep, provide no other form of income. And, of course, the revenue is even more frequent than on forestry.

2004 proved a complete conundrum. For Scottish grouse it was a disaster, yet many North of England Moors enjoyed a record season, followed by a largely disappointing 2005. The Game Conservancy Trust have two grouse research projects taking place (in the North of England and Scotland) which will hopefully show a way forward.

THE GROUSE SHOOT

There are three forms of grouse shooting - driven, walked-up and over dogs (or dogging). Scotland is, of course, the country most associated with grouse, though interestingly many of the most prolific shoots have always been in the North of England – Yorkshire, Durham and Northumberland. There are also one or two good moors in Derbyshire. Grouse are also to be found in Wales, and there are a few in Ireland.

While driven grouse shooting is without doubt very expensive, walked-up and dogging both offer excellent value. Walking-up takes the form of a line of guns (six to eight or more) walking a moor, while dogging is shooting over pointers (the dog handler and two, or perhaps three, guns). Driven grouse is very exciting and testing shooting – quite different from anything else. But walking the moors also has an appeal of its own. It's a very natural and stimulating exercise (in all senses of the word!).

DRIVEN GROUSE

It is thought that grouse were first driven in Yorkshire quite early in the nineteenth century (rumour has it that it was by a farmer and his sons). By the second half of the century the practice had spread and huge bags were being achieved – none larger than Lord Walsingham's, who accounted for 1,070 to his own gun at Blubberhouse Moor on 30 August 1888 (he used two lines of beaters). These increased bags (though 1,070 was not typical!) were largely due to the fact that driven shooting was not only a much more effective method of achieving a large bag, the densities of grouse populations had increased and shooting had thinned out the old stock. Moor owners also realised the benefits of healthy young heather.

Though it must be said that the sport is still expensive, in those days it really was exclusive. Lord Walsingham himself became bankrupt as a result of his shooting expenditure, some of it admittedly due to extravagant hospitality when playing host to the Prince of Wales (later King Edward VII), who was accustomed to a style beyond most men. Today it attracts a much wider social bracket, and it is immensely popular with overseas visitors, notably from America, Germany, Holland, Belgium, and France.

While the people have changed, the nature of driving grouse and presenting them over the butts has altered little in 100 years. A line of beaters will walk a moor in from a mile or two, or even four or five miles back. It can be a long wait in the butts, but often the birds will start to arrive in dribs and drabs before the intervals become shorter and the hectic activity starts. Flankers with flags will stop the birds flying out the side. In fact, grouse shooting is a very labour-intensive operation. Apart from 24–30 beaters, there will be four to six flankers, pickers-up and keepers, plus the game cart.

Depending on the position of your butt,

The birds approach – head down, muzzles up, and keep perfectly still.

you may be able to see a long way out front or you may not. If you have a good view it is fascinating seeing the grouse lift, then disappear from view, as they approach. On re-emerging from a dip they may have taken an entirely different course, and another bird will catch you by surprise which has similarly taken a turn. If you are unsighted, you may get some help from a whistle, as either a flanker or beater sounds an advancing bird.

Preparation

Before contemplating any shooting, the first and most important point is to gather your bearings. Take your position in the butt.

Look forward to where the birds will be coming from, then look down the line on either side. The line of butts may well be on a slope, so that those to your right are down from you, and you may only be able to see the top of one on the left – the remainder are unsighted. Much is made of it, but there can be no underemphasising the importance of safety on a grouse shoot.

Added to your positional problems, the birds themselves fly at all sorts of heights, including very low through the line. Never at any point turn with a mounted gun. If you don't hit the bird in front, take the gun out of your shoulder and, with muzzles still pointing upwards, turn and shoot behind (remembering, of

The grouse fly past the front of the butt and a loader holds a second gun ready. You really have to be on your toes.

course, the position of the picker-up). It's not as complicated as it sounds – just plain old common sense.

Taking the Shot

This is sport which really gets the adrenalin flowing. The birds will appear as if from nowhere – but you will be ready. Always keep your gun pointing forward, perhaps holding it while resting on the front wall of the butt. But keep still if you want birds to fly in your direction. You should also, incidentally, remember to reload by turning your gun sideways and pointing forwards so that you don't have to point it at your feet in the butt (a nasty accident could happen).

You will be on alert as a bird approaches. If unsighted, your neighbour may give a whistle, and if it is a low flier, mount and shoot nice and early. Be positive. This style of shooting is in total contrast to pheasant shooting. The beaters will be out of sight and quite safe. As the bird is low it will not be easy to shoot it overhead, so take it well out in front where the shot pattern will have had a chance to establish itself.

A covey will probably present itself. Think of nothing other than one bird. Be determined. Mount smoothly and quickly, on to it and shoot. And for goodness sake keep your head down on your stock. Only after you have shot the first one should you ever start to think about another. This may well be closer, so swing through and shoot the second instinctively.

If the process is too quick for the second shot, remember to take the gun from your shoulder, hold it upright with the action towards your face, keep your eyes on the bird, mount on to it, track very briefly, then through and shoot. A skilled double-gun shot will take two in front, receive the second gun from his loader and take two more out of the covey behind. You can even see skilled single-gun men do this – when taking two birds in front, they have two cartridges between the fingers of their left hand, and after shooting quickly, swing round, reload, and shoot a pair behind. These sort of tricks are fine when properly executed by extremely skilled and experienced shots, but don't try it yourself – you'll probably make a fool of yourself and put someone's life in danger as a result.

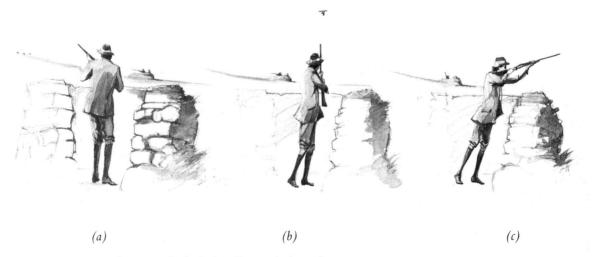

(a)   *(b)*   *(c)*

Driven grouse: (a) picking out a bird which will cross the line of guns; (b) gun out of the shoulder and turning; (c) now, having followed the bird, mount and take the shot.

Some Problems

Don't dwell on misses – if you do you will probably have several that leave you baffled. Just concentrate solely on each and every shot – each one may well be different to the last. There will be high birds, low birds, angled, coveys, ones and twos, and if there's a wind blowing they will be flying like bullets. Take each one on its merits. Don't think that because you shot the last one in a certain way, you will do the same on the next – it might be completely different.

It is also important to remember where you dropped your birds. Pickers-up on moors tend to have very good dogs, but there are days when there is little scent and there is nothing more annoying than the whole line having to wait while you try to explain to the handler in which direction your bird fell, when in truth you have no proper idea.

A grouse butt is also no place for an unaccompanied, inexperienced shot. If you find yourself standing next to one, keep an eye on him, give him firm advice and tell him to keep it simple, that is, only shoot in front.

Your clothing will play a significant role in your success. Nice, subdued gear is essential, and regardless of the weather, take a coat. It can be warm when you step out of your hotel in the morning, but by the time you reach 1,800ft (550 metres) some five miles away there might be cold wind (with a few hail stones for good measure). On the other hand, you may not need it, so ensure that your other clothes are of suitable colours. Keep a still, lowish profile as the birds approach – if you stand upright and move about you may get little shooting.

Another important accessory is a midge repellant. Moorland midges can ruin a grouse shooting expedition. They are voracious

Grouse shooting on a drizzly day with low cloud and poor visibility. Take the bird well in front.

drinkers of human blood and will drive you to distraction. Comfortable footwear is also important. Boots are the order of the day. While you may be driven to the drive, there might still be a difficult walk to the butts – the moor can be rocky and soggy too.

WALKING-UP

This may well be the cheap cousin of grouse shooting, but I love this form of shooting. There is a special magic on the tops, walking miles in the heather. It can be hard going, hot, sticky, difficult underfoot and physically exhausting, but it also offers a rare exhilaration. You walk in marvellous open landscapes

that offer no sign of human habitation, although every now and then your eye catches a distant valley, or lake. Lost in this world of wonder, your senses are shaken as a cry of cok-ok-ok fills the air from a few yards in front of you.

Brought back to reality, you throw the gun to your shoulder (or somewhere near!) and pull the trigger. The birds fly on. You open your gun, reload, turning to your neighbour and cursing, only to see another get up. This time you shoot more carefully, and just as you connect with the bird, another is alongside and you complete a right and left. It's a feat that wouldn't impress the seasoned shot, but it offers an almighty thrill. The seasoned shot would always look to shoot the

Walking-up grouse, a young bird jumps. Safety is a prime consideration.

birds that rise first and furthest. These are the oldest. The young ones are the last to leave.

One of the most important aspects of walking-up is again dressing for the job. It is also one of the most difficult. Seek the advice of your host on this one. It will be cooler on the tops, but after 30 minutes walking you will be getting hot. Boots are also important. It's sweaty work in wellies – and not at all comfortable. I'm not normally a great fan of cartridge belts, but this is one occasion where they come in handy, as does a game bag.

You must also have the ability to listen to your host and organiser. For the sake of both safety and better shooting, a straight line is a must at all times. Also observe carefully the pace of the line – your host may at certain times wish to slow it down, so as to flush the grouse gradually, rather than all at once. Birds will sometimes rise quite unexpectedly, while at other times the dogs in your line will have given some indication of their presence.

My advice on gundogs is to leave them at home unless you are totally confident of their reaction to the heather and the whole situation. I have seen normally well-behaved dogs become virtually uncontrollable. If you check with the organiser beforehand, he may well tell you that he has already arranged dogs for the day.

As for the actual shooting, it is again a question of keeping your cool and giving yourself time. Your shots will most likely be instinctive, but don't rush your gun mounting – it only takes a couple of seconds to do it properly. Similarly, don't simply poke at the birds. Remember, a grouse will rise and just as quickly drop or bank away to follow the lie of the land, so measure it a little and, again, keep your head down.

The element of surprise is probably the one key factor which finds most people out. The rushed shot which follows can never be relied upon – successful gun mounting is difficult if you hastily throw your gun to your shoulder in mid-stride. Remember the rules about footwork – body facing the direction of the grouse, weight on the front foot and gun

Grouse shooting – walking-up. It is important to keep a straight line.

Walking-up – get in a position so that the weight is on your front foot.

smoothly into the shoulder.

Try, if possible, to take the older, first bird, but when a covey gets up you will do better to settle for one particular bird, and sorting out the senior citizen can perhaps be forgotten. As the day draws on, the likely patches and peat hags from which the birds will rise become more obvious, but your limbs will grow tired and after a longish quiet spell, you will still be caught out now and again.

At night the hotel bar will be a pretty quiet place. If sleep is a problem after a day's walking-up, you really have serious insomnia

– or you are fitter than you have a right to be. On a serious note, however, it is worth taking some exercise before heading for the hill, as walking-up can be very physically demanding, and you will get much more out of it if you are in decent shape.

DOGGING

This differs from walking-up in as much as there will be a dog handler with a couple of pointers or setters, and he will be accompanied by two guns. Again, it is an inexpensive form of grouse shooting, though not so easy to find. It is also a marvellous way of conducting your sport.

Pointers and setters have been around since the seventeenth century and were originally used to point birds for netting, then for the crossbow and hawking, and finally the gun. This was the way of things until the entire shooting scene was changed by the arrival of the breech-loading shotgun in the middle of the nineteenth century.

The handler leads the way and the guns will most likely follow steadily in his wake as he allows his dogs systematically to work the ground in front and either side of him. They will cover huge areas, leaving no stem of heather to chance. They stop the instant they get the scent of a grouse, and elegantly point their head in the direction of the bird. Given the right scenting conditions, the distance can be as much as 150 yards (137 metres). Usually it is closer, and the handler will invite the guns to move in carefully either side of him and walk slowly towards the dog.

The guns will be ready to shoot as the dog eventually presses forward and flushes the birds. You don't get a lot of shooting, so you

The pleasure of a good retrieve on a warm late summer's day on the grouse moor. But is your dog up to it?

Shooting over dogs, taking care with each shot.

really make your shots count, remembering the importance of smooth and correct mounting.

It really is a fascinating day's sport. And while the walking and fresh air are tiring, generally the exercise is not so exhausting as walking-up. You spend quite a lot of time standing watching the dogs work the heather, though admittedly you'll still walk a pretty long way.

OTHER HIGH-COUNTRY SPECIES

Other high-country species include blackcock and ptarmigan.

Blackcock

With a season from 20 August to 10 December, the blackcock is now only a quarry species in isolated places. Numbers have become so sparce generally. The bird is extremely distinctive, with its split, fluted tail. The female (the greyhen) is, however, somewhat similar in appearance to the grouse. They were once found as far south as Hampshire, but are now restricted to Wales and Northern England, and predominantly Scotland, as well as several Northern European countries, Russia and Poland.

The bird is to be found on the edges of moorland where wooded areas are accessible.

Spectacular scenery as a pointer works the heather.

They are not present in sufficient numbers to be organised effectively for driven sport (and they are also a little too awkward). They present a very challenging shot, their size and powerful glide deceiving the gun into thinking that they are travelling much slower than they are. In fact, numbers are now so low that moor owners fine anyone who shoots them.

Ptarmigan

From 12 August to 10 December, the ptarmigan is a different kettle of grouse altogether, generally preferring much higher ground than usual. It also has a white plumage during the winter. A lot of romance is often attached to the pursuit of ptarmigan. It can involve a party of guns taking to remote rocky areas at the side of mountains. The bird will sit tight, then fly swiftly out from underneath the guns swinging round the mountain. It is not an easy shot, and is often missed over the top.

Parties seldom shoot more than a few brace. One is enough to make an individual's

trip worthwhile. He will take it home and have it mounted to remind him of the magic moment – and why not?

Capercaillie

Until their relatively recent withdrawal from the quarry list these were the biggest of game-birds in Britain. They are found across Northern Europe, but in Britain they are exclusive to East Central Scotland and the Highlands.

The male will weigh close to 9lb and favours the Scots pine woods, where it feeds on the needles, shoots and buds of these trees. It's a big bird with a deceptive flight and stories of a caper flying the full length of a line of guns and emerging unscathed are quite common. They were not generally present in sufficient numbers to drive, but, nevertheless, occasional drives during a day were organised. Continental sportsmen were prepared to pay good money for a bird.

7 PARTRIDGE

ENGLISH AND RED-LEG

It is a sunny October morning. The air is clean, the stubble has been ploughed into the earth, odd bits poking through erratically. The colours blend perfectly. The big hedge in front still has that rich green of late summer before giving way to the russets and browns of fall. There are big blackberries hanging among the leaves – they look so tempting, but I know that I will regret taking a step forward to pluck one. The blue of the sky, the green of the hedgerow, and golden brown of the straw-specked soil – it all looks so good.

I have been standing a little while, tentatively waiting for what may or may not be about to happen. I am wearing a Barbour and getting warmer by the minute. Just as I decide to take it off, a whistle is blown on the other side of the hedge. A covey is in the air. Muzzles up, weight forward and two birds appear in front. As I move to shoot, I thankfully realise that they are late young pheasants, still to grow their tail feathers. How embarrassing that would have been. And then the real thing – a covey of twelve or fifteen birds is bursting over the hedge in front of me.

'Pick one out,' I tell myself, 'Ignore the others.' I follow my instructions. The gun is up and into my shoulder, I am on to the bird and it has folded. Quickly onto another, it's more to my side, swing through well in front and . . . a right and left. My day has just started but is already complete . . .

Partridge shooting has become a tale of two birds – English (or grey) and red-leg (the Frenchman). The grey partridge is, of course, one of the original English gamebirds and not an import, unlike the red-leg. Once was the time when the grey partridge reigned supreme as a gamebird, and some shoots even regarded

pheasants as vermin. Red-leg have still to be properly accepted in some quarters.

There is no doubting that the attractive little grey really has an appeal of its own. Many sportsmen are unaware that it is also the slowest flier of our principal game species (32 m.p.h., unassisted by wind), for it presents itself, as if out of the blue to the unsuspecting gun, over the tops of hedgerows and will seldom fly in a straight line, but in a bewildering covey and twisting in flight.

The bad news is that its population has been in decline for some years now, following the pattern of monoculture that has robbed the partridge of its beloved hedgerows and headlands. Not only that, as the chicks are entirely dependent on insects for the first two weeks of their life, the chemical sprays with which all crops are treated effectively give young partridges precious little chance of survival. It's hard to get by without any food.

The Game Conservancy Trust (with the considerable drive and enthusiasm of Hampshire farmer Hugh Oliver Bellasis) promoted the Gamebird and Cereals Project which encourages selective spraying, urging farmers to keep the sprays away from an area of headland around their crops. Early results showed a marked improvement in the success of breeding pairs, not to mention a big return of a variety of other interesting wildlife, notably butterflies. Now the GCT are also running a hugely successful partridge recovery programme based on a project involving several adjoining farms at Royston, Herts.

The red-leg, on the other hand, is not so widely spread as a wild species in Britain, but in certain conditions it has tended to adapt much better. Though affected by drastic farming changes like everywhere else, East Anglia still has enough hedgerow and light

Plenty of partridges on this downland shoot. Note the screen behind which the guns have been crouching.

soils to provide a suitable home. Red-legs have an aversion to the wet, and with their tendency to run will pick up mud like a magnet until they reach a point when their feet are so heavy that they can barely fly at all.

It is this tendency to run (which affects most gamebirds, but especially the red-leg) which has attracted so much disdain. Yet properly presented as a driven bird, the red-leg is an excellent sporting quarry. Slightly bigger than the Englishman, it also has a straighter but faster flight. And the big plus with red-legs is that rather than flying over the guns in big packs (a habit of the grey), they come over in ones, twos and threes. Consequently, sport will be more evenly spread, and the bird lends itself well to good returns on the total released.

Often regarded as a newcomer to the game scene, the red-leg was already well established in Britain by the middle of the eighteenth century. Clearly more than a few shoots have been able to appreciate the advantages of a stock of red-legs. And unlike the grey partridge, which has a tendency to wander, red-legs are more likely to remain within the area of release. The presence of the Frenchman does not affect the stock of English; there is room for both. Of course, we would all like nothing more than to see our countryside alive with English partridges once again, but at present this seems very unlikely. And we

93

can be grateful for the sport offered by the red-leg.

DRIVEN

While the partridge season starts on 1 September, most shooting is unlikely to get under way until one month later. There are now many more shoots releasing red-legs, so partridge invitations are not the rarity that they had become. Nevertheless if you get the opportunity, cancel all other arrangements and accept. You will not regret it.

It is exciting sport and often a real test of nerve. The birds fly fast and both low and high, and if likened to anything it can be a lowland version of grouse! You will need your wits about you, the shooting will be quick, and you will need to be positive. You will also need to be careful as the birds can come low through the line and, like grouse, there is a tendency to follow them. The exception to this are those

Driven partridge – at the ready for a covey about to burst through the hedgerow.

shoots which are able to take advantage of valley drives. Famous shoots such as Gurston Down near Broadchalke and Dulverton in Somerset present high valley birds that are an altogether different proposition.

Some smaller shoots will also try to find a tall area off which to present birds. The high fliers can be quite awkward, for quite different reasons from the hedgerow hoppers. First, let's look at the classic partridge drive, with coveys bursting over tall hedgerows.

Partridges are very sensitive to noise and if they have an inkling that something is amiss, they will find a hole in the line of beaters. Indeed, a day's partridge shooting can be a nightmare for a keeper who is trying to control an inexperienced line of beaters and flankers. There will inevitably be a proportion of the birds which will run to a corner of the field which is being driven, taking to the wing only at the last minute and making their escape. The first rule, therefore, is to be quiet, and that includes from the moment of stepping out of the vehicles. Don't slam the car door. Quickly make your way to your peg. Have a look round to get your bearings, remove your gun from its slip and load up. Partridges may well be close at hand and as soon as they hear your arrival they'll be gone. The keeper will not be pleased, and quite understandably so.

Having loaded your gun, try to maintain total concentration on the area in front of you. Again, check the position of your neighbours and also any picker-up that may be behind you. A whistle is often used by the keeper or one of his line to indicate that birds are on their way over the guns. You may also hear or see the flanker waving his flag - another signal that birds are about to appear.

As soon as they appear, pick one bird out over your muzzles, move the stock smoothly into your shoulder, through the bird and shoot. You will then have an oppportunity for a second bird which, unless you are very quick, will most likely by now be overhead or perhaps to your side. If it's overhead, remember to push through when you shoot.

Taking a bird well in front, so there will be time for a second shot.

Don't just poke and hope. If the bird is to your side, as opposed to up in the air and to your side, take the gun out of your shoulder, but with muzzles still in the air, and turn leaving it until it gets behind. Double-checking on the picker-up, put your eyes closely on your intended bird, mount and push through (you will most likely have to give the bird a little 'sideways' lead, that is, shoot at the place to which it is heading).

If the bird is pricked, and no picker-up is at hand, watch carefully where it lands. A partridge can glide quite a long way and be difficult to locate on plough – but it may well die the instant it lands. Then turn and reload. Don't dwell on any misses. Think positively.

95

Partridge burst into view, springing the gun into action. Be aggressive but controlled in taking your shot.

Because of the fact that these birds are fast but low fliers, you are shooting them in front. It is therefore important to hold the gun with the muzzles up; you then merely pick your bird, mount, and push through while pulling the trigger. And don't forget the footwork. You will see people get in all sorts of muddles when partridge shooting – the fact that birds appear quickly has a panicking effect. It is so easy to forget to move your body round, but instead shoot at what will prove a very awkward angle. The art, as with all shooting, is to make each shot as easy as possible. A little thought, taking only a couple of seconds, will do that for you.

High partridges are a different ball game altogether. Driven off steep valleys, unless you are an extremely experienced shot, you will not shoot these birds in front. It is better to let them come towards you, and take them in the classic driven pheasant style. There is then a better opportunity to assess range, speed, etc., and a nice smooth swing as the bird approaches overhead will achieve the required effect. Remember to be bold with your swing. Don't try to be too precise or you will find that you will freeze and the swing will stop. Remember the shot string, and that it is better to miss in front. Again take one shot at a time.

Driven partridge – a high bird can be a very testing shot.

WALKED-UP

The partridge is not the easiest bird for walking-up. In fact, it is quite difficult to get within shooting range of a covey of partridges. This has not always been the case, for the grey partridge was once present in sufficient numbers that walking-up was a fundamental part of the shooting scene. However, with the sad decline in the Englishman's numbers, and the red-leg's liking for running rather than flying, walking-up is not a particularly fruitful proposition.

Certainly all the important factors of walking-up really come into play – walking into the wind, stealth and fieldcraft. If you are fortunate enough to get the opportunity of walking some September or October stubbles which you know hold a covey or two of partridge, then you are sure to enjoy it.

Most exercises which are demanding are all the more rewarding when successful. So it is with partridge shooting. When a covey presents itself in front of you, it is obviously important that you take advantage of the situation. You may be in the company of others, and there may be other safety factors to consider, so make a quick assessment, then concentrate exclusively on one bird. Don't hastily throw up the gun and shoot. Mount

97

Holding the gun in an alert position so as to be ready for a bird to spring into the air.

Walked-up partridge – give yourself a couple of seconds to get a good shooting stance.

smoothly, track your bird and moving the gun according to the direction of its flight, pull the trigger. Then move on to another if you can.

Again, remember footwork and keep your weight forward. The bird will fly away low in front of you so it is important that you keep your head down and your barrels nicely

into the quarry. If you have arranged maybe half a dozen guns, then you can perhaps sort out a little walking and driving between you. A bird may well fly back over your head, especially if you keep still and keep your head down. A driven shot on a walked-up shoot is a nice bonus. Another must is a dog to accompany you, preferably obedient.

8 WILDFOWL

DUCKS AND GEESE

The regular game shot will get the odd chance of either a spot of duck or goose shooting. He may well find that, much to his surprise, he becomes quite hooked on the sport. It all depends whether his invitation is to ambush a heavily fed duck pond or to tackle wild flighting mallard and widgeon, or maybe to get to grips with a muddy creek in pursuit of a pinkfoot.

There has been a trend of late for pheasant shoots to conclude the day with a visit to the farm duck pond. What ensues bears little relation to sport. The duck are invariably overfed and quite tame, they show an extreme reluctance to fly, at first presenting simple shots, but then circling to become quite difficult. Many guns in this situation do not know when to stop shooting and the consequence is a number of wounded birds that will most likely go unpicked.

The fowler seldom thinks in terms of numbers. His sport is in actually getting under the quarry and pulling off one or two good shots. He will face adversity to get there and the pleasure of bringing down one goose is ample reward for his efforts.

Admittedly there is some very good inland duck shooting – I mention the 'pond bashers' merely as a warning. A number of commercial shoots do this merely to top up the bag. They guarantee showing the birds to the guns with a minimum of effort.

A properly conducted duck shoot is excellent sport. There are four principal duck quarry species, mallard being by far the most popular. The mallard is not only the number one choice for release on private ponds and lakes, it is also the most widespread wildfowl. The truly wild birds that flight the lonely marshes and waterways of Britain, and all around the coastline, are strong, powerful fliers and a fine challenge to the sportsman. The mallard feeds by night and rests by day. It loves stubbles and spoiled potatoes.

Others which will find their way into the bag include teal, pintail and wigeon. There are also some that are easily confused with protected species. It is well worth consulting a book such as the BASC's *Handbook of Shooting* in order to know what is on the list and what isn't. Such a book will also fill in much fascinating background information.

One man and his duck – a good shot will be savoured.

The teal is a very much smaller bird than the mallard, and has an ability to rise vertically from a pond at great speed. A simulation of this flight is much used at clay pigeon shoots where it is called 'Springing Teal'.

The wigeon has given birth to many happy memories and the accompanying evocative stories of shooting under the light of the moon. It is a swift-flying bird, mostly migratory, and a challenging quarry.

The pintail adorns many sporting prints where its good looks and distinctive long, pointed 'pin' tail make it a natural subject for artists. Again, it is mostly migratory, and much more of a marsh and estuary bird than the other three.

INLAND DUCK

This takes two forms – flighting in morning or evening, or driven as part of a day's pheasant shooting. Indeed, there are some shoots offering complete days of driven duck. The opening day of the shooting season for most people who shoot is 1 September. Grouse is limited by its cost, while partridge is no longer available in sufficient numbers and nowadays may not be ready for another month.

So, it's aflighting we will go on 1 September. Whether it's ponds, drains, marshes, lake or foreshore, there is a likelihood of good sport, for the mallard is quite a testing quarry. Many folk will have been feeding their chosen spot, perhaps with some barley. It's surprising not only how much duck can eat, but also how quickly they devour it.

It is also a good idea to do a spot of reconnaissance on the days running up to the season. You will then get an idea of where the duck have been feeding and where they will tend to fly to. Whether it's morning or evening, try to get there in good time so that you are in position for the arrival of the birds, maybe from off the stubble or feeding on spoiled potatoes which have been left on a field. A few decoys in your chosen area of water will help. These can be bought at any local gunshop. But the key prerequisite is to wear clothing which will offer good camouflage, and to be still and well hidden when the birds arrive.

I live on the edge of the fens, so do a little drain shooting where there would appear to be virtually no cover whatsoever. Yet it is surprising how a place can be found among the long grasses. Try to get yourself in position so that not only are you well concealed, but you also have the benefit of decent visibility.

The biggest mistake in all duck shooting is to attempt to take your bird too early when the bird is too high. Leave it. Chances are you will miss and scare others away. It is better to keep absolutely still and give the birds complete confidence to come in to settle among your decoys.

All duck can give problems to shooters of any level of ability. The problem is that they are almost always travelling faster than they appear. Their large wing-span and plumpish body will traverse a sky backdrop which offers nothing to give any indication of range. If you are crouching on a bank or behind a bush then obviously footwork may prove a little difficult. However, apply the usual theory, that is, shoot with your body facing the correct direction, and mount on to the bird.

I personally find that duck, perhaps more than any other bird, need shooting deliberately. By that I mean that it is best to avoid any instinctive tendencies that you may have. Birds that are curling and dropping in the half light will not be hit by a gun that is fired as soon as it hits the shoulder as regularly as one which has tracked the bird before swinging through and shooting.

As one who has to curb his tendencies to shoot instinctively, I speak from bitter experience. Most landing duck are missed over the top and behind. A controlled but positive swing through the bird on to its projected flight line should do the trick.

Mallard lift off the pond.

The gun was hidden by a hedge as the duck came off a lake. Think of safety first.

If you are shooting with a pal who cannot resist the temptation to have a go at the high birds, tell him to stop as soon as possible. Explain that once these birds feel safe to land then he will have a much better chance of shooting one. Patience really is a great virtue.

Some ponds and marshes very thoughtfully provide hides. Shooting in such places is very civilised and there is no excuse for not applying good technique. The same rules apply. Keep down and well hidden until the birds are confident enough to drop in from their reconnaissance zone. You can then stand, and with weight on your front foot, pick first one bird, and then another.

The teal is a quarry which presents a quite unorthodox target for the game shot. Rising sharply and going away, the man who is used to driven pheasant will very often miss it underneath and to one side. For starters, contrary to what your eyes may tell you at a glance, very few teal rise at a perfect vertical from your standing position. They are mostly veering to one side or the other. So don't hurry the shot. Be sharp and positive with your mounting, but get on to the bird's flight and swing smoothly through the bird, shooting on the swing.

With both dropping mallard and springing teal there is a tendency to raise the head to 'make sure' at the point of taking the shot. This will serve no other purpose than to give you a bruise on your cheek and a couple of wasted cartridges.

In the half-light in which you will most likely be shooting, coupled with perhaps the most awful weather (torrential rain has a habit of accompanying my sorties to the water's edge) this quick look 'to be sure' is hard to hold in check. But hold it you must.

Finally, for any form of flighting, there are two musts – safety and a dog. With birds that are dropping on to water, you must remember your safety zones. Somebody may be on the other side of the pond from you. Similarly, never entertain the idea of going duck shooting unaccompanied by a gundog. A wounded mallard can fly quite a long way before landing, and there's nothing worse than leaving a hit bird. To that end, make sure that you also have a good torch with you for the evening flight.

Driven duck require very similar tactics to high pheasants. It is basically all down to stance, footwork, mounting and the smooth swing through the bird. But remember that the bird will be travelling faster than you think, so push through a little more. Again, don't be tempted to pull off shots in extreme range. Duck that are flushed from a pond may circle a couple of times in the hopes that they can return to their spot of water. Their height will be increasing and your neighbour might pull off an incredible shot. This will mean little – it was probably a fluke. If you observe one or two others attempting such shots, you will see that birds are being pricked, a most unsatisfactory state of affairs.

Springing teal – the birds lift sharply.

A dog is an essential companion for all duck shooting sorties.

Making the retrieve.

FORESHORE DUCK

We here enter the realms of the seasoned fowler. This is a craft all of its own and there is no quick short-cut to harnessing the experience needed in order to get the most out of a visit to the foreshore, be it under the moon, or the dawn or evening flights. Low expectations in terms of bag should figure highly on the list of priorities. Other important aspects are an accompanying gundog, permission to shoot the relevant strip of foreshore, careful thought as to where you position yourself and perhaps most importantly, some pretty rough weather.

A warm still evening is bad news for the fowler. He wants a stiff wind to keep the birds down and within range. Conversely, however, an extended run of poor weather in January and February (the season continues until 20 February below the sea wall) will cause the birds to lose condition. A statutory ban may come into force, but if conditions are such, wildfowlers will mostly have halted their shooting by this time.

You will get the most out of foreshore shooting by accompanying someone in the know. He cannot be certain of putting you under duck, but he will be able to put the odds in your favour. He will know the tides, the creeks and the likely flight lines. As chances are seldom numerous you will want to make each shot count. Many like to use a big magnum on the foreshore, combined with tight chokes for those long-range shots.

In actual fact, your own game gun should be fine. And it is in instances such as this that multi-chokes are an advantage. You can use your normal gun, but this time stepping up the choke a little. Several modern wildfowlers favour semi-automatic shotguns. As this type of shooting is a solitary sport, there is seldom anyone present who can object, and as the auto is easier to load in a confined space, there is a very good argument for these guns. These too have multi-chokes.

The whole question of choke and load for foreshore duck is a never-ending source of debate (*see* Chapter 3). Whatever your combination, a tight choke and a magnum gun alone will not shoot your quarry – they must be pointed in the right place. The tendency of knowing you have some extra hitting power up your sleeve is subconsciously to let it do the work for you.

In fact, you need to be on your toes more than ever when wildfowling. For starters, judging range is extremely important – don't be tempted to shoot out-of-range birds. Similarly, if you try what you feel is a good longish shot, remember to keep as still as possible until the moment of mounting on to the bird, swinging through its line to shoot. Be confident and relaxed enough to swing well through before pulling the trigger, keeping the swing going.

There is great satisfaction to be had from a single bird on the foreshore.

There can be no underestimating the importance of concealment when wildfowling. Never move until the shot is to be taken.

Well before shooting, if your position doesn't allow you to stand at least remember to face the point at which you expect to take your shot, that is, the easiest point. And keep your head well down. Make sure that you also know the tides – don't find yourself up a creek with neither canoe nor paddle! Seriously, there are many warnings given but the danger of tides cannot be overstressed.

GEESE

With the ever-expanding population of Canada geese there is now quite a lot of inland goose shooting taking place under very similar circumstances to duck flighting. This varies, but can be quite unsporting, with big geese shot at close ranges as they either lumber off water or are taken coming into it. Shot selectively and sensibly, however, the Canada has a deceptively fast flight and offers some good shooting. And, in many areas, the Canada has now reached pest proportions, causing considerable damage to land and crops.

Greylags and pinkfeet, the Scandinavian migrants, are mostly what fowlers refer to as geese for shooting. Like the geese themselves, fowlers will travel miles and endure terrible conditions. Hour after hour, night after night, they will sit in a cold, wet muddy creek, waiting and hoping. They will also frequently go home empty-handed, but seldom despair – they know that one bird will make it all worthwhile.

There are several goose shooters who like to bring out their big bore guns – and be it a 10 or an 8 bore, what fascination they hold. The long barrels and extra shot charge are seen to be 'gun' enough for those long-range, big birds that will need a good pattern of big

shot to bring them down. However, the usual rules of shooting apply – if you use one of these guns, they need to be mounted and swung with the same care and precision as an ordinary 12. Admittedly the long barrels and extra weight can help give that bit of extra swing and forward allowance, but you will still need to do everything else as normal. Don't bank on your extra firepower.

My advice for anyone looking for some goose shooting is to go with a reputable guide. There are one or two rogues in the game (as in everything else) but there are also some very good ones. Also, your local wildfowling club is sure to be of assistance and most are only too glad to help newcomers and anyone looking to get more seriously involved in wildfowling. The only problem now is that there are waiting lists for membership of several of the better clubs. It will also be worthwhile contacting the BASC.

The greylags are far away over the loch.

Alan Murray puts the call into action.

The geese have swung round and are close.

Alan gets to his feet and picks out his bird.

Three or four years ago I spent a couple of days with Alan Murray in Fife. I was particularly lucky as not only is Alan an excellent goose guide, but also present in the party was one of the best known guides of them all, Peter Blackburn of the Solway. It was an enlightening stay. Our shooting was based around two lochs, but nowhere near any of the roostings – Alan stressed the importance of this.

Patience really is a virtue with geese, particularly on an evening flight. A few small, earlier groups will offer tempting shooting, and the background bugling crescendo from birds getting ready to lift into the sky really raises the pulse rate. They call it goose fever, and it's hard to contain yourself – but one early shot can ruin the entire flight. The birds are much easier spooked than shot!

Concealment can be difficult on the foreshore. It is vital to keep completely still until on the point of taking the shot.

If all guns (perhaps five or six under a guide's supervision) wait until the big skeins have lifted, everyone may get off a couple of shots – perhaps four if they are quick to reload. The evening flight is generally over fairly quickly, but the sight and sound of so many geese taking to the air is an experience never to be forgotten. You don't get a big bag, and you won't need one either to stir the excitement or the memory.

Morning flights tend to last rather longer as smaller skeins take turns to lift off the water. A call and sometimes decoys can be used to good effect, but you need to know how it's done.

You must weigh up your own options with regard to gun, choke and cartridge. Alan Murray uses an over-under 12 bore choked ¼/½ with 1½oz (43g) cartridges of No. 3 shot (or 4). While there are many who favour a BB or No. 1 shot, technical argument would tend to favour the denser pattern achieved by a load of No. 3.

The rules for shooting geese are very much the same as high pheasant. And certainly don't attempt to take a bird well in front. Range judging is also very important. Be sure that your chosen bird is within range, for a wounded goose can plane irretrievably for a great distance. Only pull the trigger if you are positive that you can bring off a good, clean kill.

Let the bird come to you, keeping incredibly still. Your crouched position in a hide, ditch or creek, may prevent orthodox footwork, but attempt to rise and shoot so that you are nicely positioned with your weight properly balanced. Take the bird as it passes directly overhead. And don't be deceived by that huge, slow wing beat. These birds are really motoring and you will need more forward allowance than you imagine, so keep that gun swinging. Think of the shot string, and forgetting the body of the goose, shoot for its head. A goose head equates to the size of a standard clay pigeon, so thinking in terms of 'head only' will help give you the lead necessary to execute a successful shot.

At the end of the morning flight.

The head of a goose compared to a clay.

109

Footwork doesn't apply, but notice how the other rules of stance come into play.

In certain circumstances it is possible to make big bags, but resist the temptation. No matter how many you shoot, you will not improve the thrill and memory of two or three birds well taken. And you will do much to harm the image of the sport. The golden rule, especially applicable to geese, is always to respect your quarry.

9 Pigeon

Maybe not a gamebird, but most definitely sporting in the truest possible sense, the woodpigeon is a favourite for thousands of shooters. The woodie is a test of both shooting skill and fieldcraft. Those who shoot decent bags with any consistency are almost always those who are reaping the rewards of years of dedication. Nobody becomes a successful pigeon shooter overnight. Those who account for big bags don't necessarily have the special land over which to shoot, but the know-how to make the most of their visits. However, it's a lot of fun learning.

The pigeon is unique in that to a farmer it really is a pest and feeding in big flocks can cause massive damage to crops. By shooting the birds you are doing the farmer a genuine favour. Indeed, in the past, farmers have been happy to give people cartridges to control the birds.

The woodpigeon is a voracious eater. Roosting in the trees by night and flying out to farmland to feed by day, it changes its appetite throughout the year to match the stocks of food available. Probably the biggest single factor to affect pigeon flocks in recent years has been the advent of oilseed rape. This is now grown in vast quantities and pigeons absolutely love it. Moreover, it offers nourishing food at a time of year when the pickings might otherwise be lean.

The bad news is that because of both pressure on the birds (more and more people are now turning to pigeon for their sport) and the wide availability of food, the pigeon has become increasingly difficult to decoy, particularly on rape where it gathers in huge flocks. A couple of shots and the birds will be gone to pastures new. Gale conditions offer the best opportunities.

There are, however, other crops on which it is still possible to make a worthwhile bag – winter drilling in the autumn, greens during the winter, plus the odd rape field (and in early spring), and freshly sown cereals in the spring. Peas and beans can be superb and laid corn is a traditional summer favourite.

Perhaps one of the most significant factors in a successful foray is reconnaissance. Having been fortunate enough to accompany one or two seasoned pigeon shooters I have found that they usually have infinite patience. I have had some very enjoyable outings with John Gray and at times we have been in the car so long that I wondered if we would ever get set up. He would go for his original chosen field, only to find the birds had flown, and that there was little left for them to feed on. After travelling miles along country lanes, frequently stopping and scanning the horizons with binoculars, he would see a few birds here and there but wouldn't abandon his quest until he found what he thought was his best chance. If he didn't already have permission to shoot the land (and through years of regular shooting, he has built up quite a patch) he would find the farmer in question and make the appropriate request, pinpointing the field where he anticipated the birds would be causing a lot of trouble. But once he had made his decision, he was seldom proved wrong. You can't have a bonanza every time, indeed, no matter how good it looks, there will always be blanks, but John mostly found us some shooting.

Many of my trips with him were in the autumn when we shot over fields of freshly sown winter wheat or barley. Pigeons are attracted like magnets to the scattered grain. Deep hedgerows also offer good cover for a hide at this time of year. Weather conditions are often ideal, with fresh but not cold winds – it is a true pleasure to be out there.

I spent another memorable day, this time in late February, with Philip Fussell, one of the finest shots I have had the pleasure to meet. Philip has done a lot of salmon fishing and game shooting over the years, but remains fanatical about his pigeon shooting, and from February through to the beginning of May will barely miss a day if he can help it.

A very modest and unassuming character, the statistics had to be drawn out of him. He will shoot around 4,000 birds during the three and a half months. His best ever day came on Salisbury Plain in 1959 when he accounted for 495. He has shot many 300s and on the two days prior to our meeting he had shot in the 130s. Sharing a hide with such a man was a fascinating experience. When I asked him the secret to his success with pigeon, he replied: 'You must remember that I have

been shooting pigeon for a long time – you tend to learn a lot'. And so you do.

Pigeon shooting really is a fascinating sport. There is, indeed, so much to learn about the ways of a pigeon – how he can be outwitted, and how it is possible to make the best of an apparently unpromising situation.

The other hugely popular method of tackling pigeon is roost shooting. The roost shoots of February and March can offer some very testing sport. The bags are seldom significant and can't generally hope to match those of decoy shoots, but it has an appeal of its own and a couple of cracking high fliers can stay in the memory for a long time.

DECOYED PIGEON

The great appeal of pigeon shooting is that it offers just about every shot in the book. Sitting in a hide you will be taking birds that drop like mallard, soar overhead like pheasants, spring into the air like teal – the list is endless. In other words, a good pigeon shot is likely to be a very good all round shot who would perform well at any kind of shooting. But to get this kind of activity in a hide you need one essential ingredient – pigeons! So how do you go about it?

As we have already discussed, a site must be chosen where there appears to be a good possibility of the presence of feeding pigeon. A previous reconnaissance will reveal whether they have found a field which has been freshly sown, or is appealing for other reasons. The birds may have been observed feeding there for the first time the previous day.

Some farmers thoughtfully anticipate trouble and provide straw bale hides, but most often you will have to make your own. So, having found the likely looking field, consider a suitable shooting position. Your hide will best be sited close to a tree. Such a position not only gives the shooter shelter from the bird's view, it also gives the pigeon confidence, as they

Philip Fussell and Philip Beasley at the end of a successful day in a pigeon hide. The springer retrieved from far and wide – all 'hit' birds were collected.

112

Getting the hide ready.

often like to land in a tree before dropping to feed. You can place a lofted pigeon decoy in the tree. This is where we enter into the realms of the pigeon shooter's paraphernalia. There is a host of equipment available to the decoy shooter, much of which is necessary for successful sport.

A net, camouflage or otherwise, should be placed around the front of the hide. Ideally you will lace it with grasses, ivy or branches, whichever is the most suitable vegetation for the position in which you are situated, to make it blend perfectly with the background. A big knife or 'slasher' is therefore a must. A level floor to the hide is also a big help, as is an empty oil drum on which to sit. A dozen or so decoys will be necessary. Most serious pigeon shooters use dead birds from a previous outing, but this a catch-22 situation – if you have not shot any on the last outing, their

provision might be somewhat difficult.

Artificial decoys are then the obvious option, and there is a wide choice available. Either full-bodied or shell (hollow) can be used, but any hint of shinyness on the paintwork will be as big a deterrent as if you were standing out there in the field without any clothes on.

Your pattern will be placed around 20 yards (18 metres) in front of the hide, with the deeks all facing into the wind at varying angles. A pigeon never feeds with its back to the wind – it doesn't like its feathers ruffled.

It can be a good idea to shape the pattern so that there is a space in the middle in which the pigeons can land. The decoys will be placed 6 feet (2 metres) or more apart. You might also like to place an artificial crow on the edge of the pattern. Crows are wary creatures but will often be seen close to feeding pigeon, and the presence of your black decoy may be just

113

Ivy leaf is taken from another tree nearby to use to camouflage the hide.

A full-bodied decoy – one with an attachment enabling it to be perched on a wire fence.

The shell decoy – light and easy to carry, but ensure that a dull paint is used. Any gleam or shine will scare off real woodies.

Add to the decoy pattern as birds are shot.

Choose a hide position near a tree, if possible. Note how the decoy pattern has already been added to by birds shot during the session.

the extra incentive needed to persuade cruising cushats (as they are known in Scotland) to drop in for a feed. You might also take a flapper, a cradle on which a dead bird can be positioned. A string is trailed from it towards the hide, so that the wings can be intermittently flapped in a realistic manner.

An optimist to the last, the pigeon shooter will have a couple of sacks with him to carry home the bag at the end of the day. And he will also have plenty of cartridges – he never

knows when the bonanza might happen. Running out of cartridges is not a lot of fun when you are in the middle of the shoot of a lifetime and four fields, two cart-tracks and ten miles of road from the nearest gunshop.

Lunch and a flask of drink are the other necessary accompaniments of a day in the hide. And you can be sure that, no matter how slack your shooting, you only have to delve into your lunch-box, take a bite of a sandwich and you will look up to see two

The most effective decoys are shot, using a stick to prop up the head – though if it gets busy you may not have time for sticks!

pigeon lift from the middle of the decoys and fly into the distance. The sandwich is dropped to the floor, the gun is grabbed, but the chance is already lost. The call of nature can have a similar effect.

The other consideration in the actual setting up of a hide is the possibility of taking shots. Can you observe the incoming pigeons without showing yourself, and if so, will it be possible to take shots at a variety of angles?

While it is necessary to build a hide that will conceal you from the tremendously keen eyesight of a woodpigeon, having drawn birds into your pattern there should be room enough to take a shot. This might be stating the obvious, but in making a hide, particularly in the bottom of a thick hedgerow, an awkward branch very often doesn't show itself until it pokes you in the back of the neck when you stand to shoot!

Is there a safe fall-out zone? Can you shoot at all angles without worrying whether you might be rattling pellets against a farm building, over a road or in the line of a tractor working in the adjacent field?

The pigeons themselves, when they start to arrive, will always land into the wind. So if the wind is blowing towards the hide, don't shoot the front bird first – the back one will have seen you rise and will turn on the wind in a split second. He will be away in no time.

Concealment is so important. If you have ever travelled in a light aircraft you will know that it is possible, even for the human eye, to see the slightest movement at long distances. The pigeon, with its 340-degree vision, detects danger at extreme range. On a sunny day the glint of gun barrels can be a real give-away. The white of a human face is a tell-tale sign at all times, so keep low. If at all possible,

You will have ensured that while the hide offers good concealment, you also have enough room to take your shots.

observe the skyline and your pattern from through the netting rather than over the top of your hide. A floppy hat is, in any event, also a help.

While you will be presented with a wide variety of shots, including some real scorchers, the people who put together the biggest bags will invariably point out that they always look to take the simplest birds. Don't be ambitious. Wait until the woodies are well within range and present good shots. Many like to let the birds settle, taking one on the ground and the other lifting, going away. Others feel ground shots give them little satisfaction, and opt to take both on the wing. Once you get a good pigeon shoot going there will be some marvellous shooting to be had, with a whole repertoire of rights and lefts. Birds winging directly over the hide can be particularly satisfying.

Obviously the rules of footwork have to be abandoned, but all other principles are every bit as applicable. A good pigeon shooter will think out his shots. Some will be quick and instinctive, others will be measured. In all instances the gun will be mounted, and the eye will never be lifted to double check the bird. The body will be in the position facing the chosen shot and the shoulder will not drop, if at all possible, as this pulls the stock away from the face. There may also be a call for shooting while sitting on the drum. With practice this comes quite naturally, but remember to keep the body forward.

Keep the barrel swing smooth and efficient. Concentrate on each and every shot and don't take any bird for granted. Two or three very good shots can easily be followed by a couple of misses on much more straightforward birds – complacency will be to blame. Taking

Stay concealed and perfectly still until ready to shoot. Note how the hat 'hides' the face.

Unless spooked, pigeon coming into roost over treetops can offer a classic driven shot.

Pigeon hide footwork. When sitting keep the right foot back to give maximum swing to the right.

two corkers will count for nothing on your next shots as the birds will most likely be completely different, and though they might appear easier, don't entertain the idea that they are.

There is much to be said for using a 20 bore in a pigeon hide. It is light and offers the quick handling so often necessary in cramped situations. Interestingly, I know that John Gray has now changed to a 26-inch over-under after many, many years using a Charles Boswell 30-inch side-by-side, while Philip Fussell also uses 30-inch barrels exclusively on his over-under. Both are good shots and found that the extra barrel length was no handicap. In fact, like all good shots, they have that knack of making a little extra time for themselves. It all goes back to doing everything properly – being positive and smooth with a good gunfit and gun mounting and taking an extra couple of seconds rather than rushing a shot.

Philip's gun was also choked full and full (as opposed to John's improved and half). He felt that the choke was particularly necessary nowadays. He modestly explained that much of his shooting was done when pigeon were a far easier proposition. Nowadays, with the advent of rape and the birds under so much pressure, they have become much more wary and harder to decoy. He felt that it was necessary to have a good, tight hard-hitting pattern for consistent kills. He acknowledged that it called for more accuracy, but this was offset by the lack of pricked birds, including those that were landing on the edge of the pattern. Both Philip and John favour 7 shot cartridges.

There was also another important factor which both had in common when putting together good bags of pigeon. They were fastidious about marking birds and would never entertain the idea of leaving the field until every shot bird was collected. Philip with his Springer, Whisky, and John with black Lab Sam were formidable retrieving teams and would, at the end of the day, collect birds from every conceivable corner of the field.

It is surprising how far a pigeon can fly, particularly on a wind, after being shot. An added advantage of shooting over an open field is that it is possible to watch where those hit birds might have pitched. For those that land behind a hedgerow, a dog should be sent as soon as possible.

Wounded birds or birds lying belly up should not be left in the shooting area. Indeed, it is best to collect all birds as soon as is reasonably possible, and place them in the pattern. The bigger the pattern the better. You can place sticks under the beaks of the earlier birds to give them a more authentic look. Later it may get too busy, but always place them as realistically as possible, and leave a good landing position for others in that part of the pattern which is relatively close to the hide.

When you finally come to leave your hide,

A bird is taken as it drops into decoys on winter drilling

John Gray on the way home after a good October afternoon's sport.

remember to clear up any litter, including all the spent cartridge cases. You may want to make a return visit, and to that end it is also a sensible idea to contact the farmer, either on the way home, or by ringing him later that evening, to let him know how you got on. He will most certainly appreciate the courtesy and he will also be interested to hear about your efficiency.

If you didn't shoot very many he will know that you kept the birds off. If you put together a big bag then he will realise what a good job you have done – and in both instances he will know who to turn to when he next has an invasion of woodies.

THE ROOST SHOOT

I must be completely honest and admit my masochistic tendencies. Despite never really accounting for what might be termed a decent bag, I love pigeon roost shooting. It can be both one of the most frustrating forms of shooting ever and also one of the

Roosting pigeons – look for favourite trees.

most satisfying.

While flight line shooting can be enjoyed the year round, most roost shooting takes place in February when the pheasant shooting season has finished and guns can now get into the woods in an attempt to thin out local flocks of woodies. Farmers know that their spring crops will otherwise be in for a hammering. Indeed, many estates hold organised shoots during February when individuals and wildfowling clubs arrive *en masse* to man all of the woods in the area. This is obviously an essential part of roost shooting, as birds will be kept on the move. They will inevitably find the one wood in which no guns are standing, but hopefully, in the mean time, they will have offered some sport on the way.

The best conditions are dull and overcast with good strong winds. Those otherwise delightful crisp, sunny February afternoons are absolutely useless for pigeon shooting. The birds, already wary after a day's feeding on rape, return to the woods at the height of a mid-Atlantic 747 (only a slight exaggeration). But land they must. So, apply all theories based on common sense. Where are they

most likely to land? Are there any signs of droppings? And can you find a suitable position which offers both concealment and the possibility of actually being able to shoot?

The woods at this time of year are without leaf and are completely bare. An ivy-clad stump may be your only concealment. Your face will be the big give-away, so stay concealed as long as possible. You will be holding your gun with muzzles up, so stand, mount, track, swing and shoot with one flowing motion. Don't snatch or poke – you will miss. Gun mounting will be very important, for the shots will not be easy, with high birds drifting over the tree-tops giving only fleeting appearances. Follow through as though the branches aren't there.

You will need to be warm, but choose thermals rather than excessive layers of coats and sweaters. Mounting the gun on the shoulder joint, with bruised, uncomfortable consequences, results from excessive clothing. So do missed shots.

You can also try putting a lofted decoy in position to draw some birds. If one or two singles pass overhead early on, it may be worth resisting the temptation of taking a shot. Watch where they are flying to and give them a chance to settle. They may draw others. If none look like pitching in and you are merely on a flight line, then swing into action. But don't shoot at out-of-range birds. Not only is it a waste of cartridges, it may well spoil the possibility of better shooting, having robbed the birds of confidence to come into your chosen wood.

You really need to keep your wits about you, for while there may well be a flight line, there will inevitably also be birds that fly from behind. Be prepared to take them going away, remembering to swing well under and to the relevant side in order to gain the necessary forward allowance. You might also find that, because of the lack of cover, other birds may be best tackled in this manner. If you stand with your back to their flight line, they will have little chance of seeing you, but

Whether roost or flight line shooting, it is important to find a position which offers concealment (that is, near a tree) but also fairly decent visibility. You really need to be on your toes.

crane your head vertically so that you have the maximum possible chance as they pass over. Such shots are quite difficult but they offer an option where there might otherwise be none.

Birds may well have landed in trees nearby that have escaped your attention, so be at the ready if you hear the distinctive clap of wings as they take to the air again.

All birds should be picked up while shooting. It can be difficult looking for fallen birds afterwards, particularly as the light seems to fade very quickly in a wood at the end of a winter's afternoon. Remembering where each bird fell is often the most difficult task. The final consideration is not to leave packing up until too late – the pheasants will want to go up to roost.

10　Other Species

WOODCOCK

The cry of 'cock' is enough to induce half a line of beaters to throw themselves on the ground. The magic of this elusive bird is such that it can encourage a normally safe shot to make an idiot of himself.

The woodcock is the almost mythical bird of long beak and silent flight which will show himself without warning on a pheasant drive. He will jink and weave in such a way as to put a spell on anyone within range. As he emerges from the trees the bird may rise, twist, or both, and sail down through the

'Woodcock forward' – don't frighten the beaters!

line. A gun looking for a quick shot may suddenly find himself either shooting low in front or swinging through the line, hence the tendency for beaters to dive for cover!

The woodcock is a bird which all sportsmen relish. He is distinctive, handsome, mysterious and a testing shot. While many, many woodcock migrate to Britain from Scandinavia, Russia and Germany in October and early November, there is a growing native breeding population in Great Britain. They have a liking for dry, deciduous woodland, with nearby damp ground for feeding. That long beak will seek out worms and insects near the surface. They also like young evergreen plantations. Consequently, many pheasant drives feature this very same cover

and as likely as not will throw up the odd woodcock, particularly as the cold weather starts to strike from November.

As a wader, but one which tends to do little wading these days, the woodcock is included in wildfowl hard weather shooting bans. Yet the woodcock is perhaps one bird which is in least need of protection, flying long distances if the weather doesn't suit. As a good friend once remarked: 'A woodcock votes with its wings.'

A right and left at woodcock is a private ambition for most shooting people. Such an achievement also entitles you to membership of the *Shooting Times* Woodcock Club, formerly the Bols Snippen Club. This feat is much more likely to be accomplished when

The woodcock.

A ride on a shoot in Hampshire which at certain times of the year lends itself to a woodcock drive.

walked-up shooting, particularly in some areas of Ireland where the bird tends to move in largish numbers. A woodcock will sit quite tight until flushed and then, as a going-away bird, is a much less demanding target than driven, its flight being less erratic and mostly contained completely to a 'safety zone'.

A woodcock on a driven shoot, however, is an entirely different proposition. He will appear without warning, and take to a direction at which it is most likely impossible to shoot. A very large percentage of birds flushed from a wood will quickly find another tree behind which they will immediately fly and the chance will be lost.

I have come close to taking a right and left. On the first occasion (in Norfolk, where many of the winter visitors arrive and stay until the weather turns nasty on them) the two birds followed an identical flight line, rising out of a wood nicely over my left shoulder. I shot one, but opened my gun briefly without seeing the second. I immediately closed it and successfully took the

second bird. But this does not count as a correct 'right and left'.

The other instance was in Hampshire. Remarkably, two birds came out of a drive together, and crossed in front of me. I could hardly believe my good fortune, but as I shot the first, the other slipped behind a clump of trees and reappeared about 60 yards away. I am resigned to the fact that I may never get another chance – but live in hope!

The woodcock, then, is a bird which stirs great excitement. The first rule is to stay cool. Quickly assess the position – is it safe, or would it be better to wait? Don't worry if you cannot get a shot in. If one woodcock has appeared there will most likely be two or three more about.

If the shot is safe, remember stance and footwork, and mounting smartly but correctly, briefly try to follow the flight line before swinging through. You will not have much time, but make the most of what you have – don't just throw the gun in the bird's general direction. You may also find that if you follow the flight it will swing round the back of the line of guns to return to the wood from which it emerged at the other end. I have taken two or three like this, including a couple which I count as probably my finest moments! You may by now have gathered that the woodcock is a real favourite.

SNIPE

The snipe is similar in many ways to the woodcock – long beak, small body with large wings, binocular vision. But put one along-side the other and the similarity ends. The snipe is Britain's smallest gamebird. Once found in huge numbers, it occasionally pro-vided driven sport on the marshes of East Anglia, Southern England and Ireland. After suffering a massive decline with the drainage of much of its favourite land, the bird now appears to be holding its own.

It loves wet splashes of any sort, mostly adjacent to cover, and probably provides best sport when walked-up. But its rapid accelera-tion as it zigzags upwards will panic the coolest of shots, even when he is stalking a bit of ground in the knowledge that it may hold a

There is always an element of surprise with snipe shooting – this is an essential part of its appeal. It springs into the air with a zigzag flight.

snipe. Instinctive shots can attempt to shoot them quickly, but mounting must be absolutely precise. Slower, more deliberate shots should perhaps measure the bird out a little. But they are easily flushed and out of range in no time, so the shot may well have to be quick.

Walking-up a hedgerow with a couple of pals I had the opportunity of a right and left one season. They got up from a wet corner of a grass field, only five yards from my feet. A hard weather ban was on at the time, however, so (despite the more recent massive thaw) I refrained from shooting. Is it better to say I could have shot them, rather than I missed them?

It is still possible to shoot driven snipe, and given the right conditions this is not uncommon in the West Country, and especially Ireland, where the bird abounds in largish numbers. In both instances the bags will be small, and the drives brief but very exciting.

It is important to find some cover. Once you are spotted by a snipe, the little bird will jink away from you in an instant. Its flight is also deceptive, but don't dwell on the bird – a nice upright stance, muzzles up, then into the bird, smoothly through and shoot. But such opportunities will be rare – your best bet is an odd shot on a rough shoot walk-about or on a grouse moor.

GOLDEN PLOVER

The other wader on the quarry list is the golden plover, a bird shot only in small numbers, although it is in no way under any long-term threat. Most are taken in the course of other game shooting, often driven.

RABBIT

One for the pot – the big days of rabbit shooting may be long gone, but there are still more than enough around to provide sport for most shooting folk who take the trouble to find permission to walk a stretch of suitable land. Ferrets and guns can make for great fun, but the flip side of all rabbit shooting is its dangerous aspect. Without wishing to be a

Standing up to a hedge for driven snipe.

Don't shoot the ferret!

bore, there have been a lot of accidents on rabbit shooting sorties – dogs, ferrets and people have all been shot. And it's not only those who are in the immediate company who are in danger. Ricocheted pellets can hit people unsighted by bushes or other cover. Many a romantic moment in the undergrowth has been spoiled when a couple's ardour has been dampened at the quick by a shot in pursuit of a bolting bunny!

Make sure all is safe. In taking the shot itself, the weight must be on the front foot, with the body leaning well into the gun which will be mounted on to the rabbit, moving smoothly through for the shot. Remember, again, that it is a good idea to think only in terms of the rabbit's head – you will then be much less likely to miss behind or wound the animal.

If a rabbit appears on a formal driven pheasant day, don't entertain the idea of shooting unless expressly permitted by your host.

HARE

Like the rabbit, the hare has suffered mixed fortunes – where once fields were heaving with hares, now there are only ones and twos. During the last couple of years or so some areas have reported an increase, but there are still many shoots which forbid the shooting of hares purely because they like to see a few about the place and their numbers are such that they cannot stand any more losses. Others forbid their shooting purely because of the danger involved. A hare will run through the line of guns on an almost suicidal course, putting not only its own life in danger, but also that of the guns. An excited shot in such instances can result in a nasty accident.

Estates and farms with enough hares have hare shoots in February which are often attended by the beaters and pickers-up who have helped during the season, and many others. To run a hare drive effectively, an army of 40 guns is often called upon, and

Rabbit shooting – the first style is not recommended, the second is the correct stance.

The hare.

keeping such a large number in order is truly an operation on a military scale for the organising keeper. Any fewer, however, and the shoot ceases to be effective. The walking line needs to cover the full width of a field. Such a shoot often takes place at the end of the season, when cock pheasants are included. The shooters are divided in half, and 20 take it in turns to stand and walk. Such days are

enormous fun, with enough banter to fill a book, and certainly fire an appetite and thirst that will later be satiated among exaggerated stories at the village local.

You'll need to keep your wits about you on these shoots, and not only in order to shoot the hares. Ancient, rusting guns are often put into use annually on these occasions, and their owners don't worry too much about unloading between drives, or in which direction the muzzles are pointing!

Hares themselves are an unusual quarry. They are viewed by many with mixed feelings – the squeal of an improperly shot hare is not a pleasant sound. So spare yourself and the hare such agonies by placing the shot in the correct place, that is, the head and not its legs and backside. In fact, unless you have a clear view of the head, it's best not taking a shot.

Virtually the same advice applies to hare shooting as to rabbit. With weight well forward the front foot and stock well mounted,

A hare shoot – when the going gets tough, you will need the right footwear.

Remember – weight forward and head tight on the stock.

You may think twice about shooting a hare early in the drive – leave it to someone else so that they can carry it through the heavy plough.

think only in terms of the head as your target. The swing through should be smooth, as with any other quarry. Be careful not to shoot off your back foot – the outcome will most likely be a shot that is behind and over the top. When the pellets hit the earth you will be reminded of your error.

Because the hare is a big animal, approximately 8lb (3·6kg) with lots of excellent meat, it is better to use 4 or 5 shot cartridges. The extra hitting power could make all the difference between a clean kill and a badly wounded animal. You may also note that

when out on an organised walked-up shoot on tough terrain, the more experienced shots will be generous in their tendency to give others the shooting. This may well have much more to do with the fact that they prefer not to be saddled with a heavy hare in their game bag for the rest of what may be an arduous day!

11   Conduct and Kit

SAFETY

Safety – arguably the most boring, and also the most important word in shooting. I may have laboured the point and most certainly this will be the least well-read section of the book, but I make no apologies.

Perhaps the five most crucial don'ts to remember are:

1.   Never point a loaded gun at anyone.
2.   Never rely on a safety catch.
3.   Never have a gun loaded unless you are in position and ready to shoot.
4.   Never be in the company of others with an unbroken gun.
5.   Never carry both 12 and 20 bore cartridges.

All five are obvious enough but one or all of them are broken at some point at most game shoots during a season.

Guns are seldom pointed at anyone deliberately, but there is always that fateful excited moment when swinging through the line on taking a shot. I remember standing in a hedgerow to the rear of two guns on a partridge drive. I whistled to both guns at the start of the drive to ensure that they knew of my whereabouts and they waved a hand of acknowledgement. A few minutes later a partridge passed between the two, down the line of the hedgerow. The gun on the right, who was 19 at the time, missed first barrel and swung on to take a second shot. He blew a pile of branches from the bush about two feet above my head! He knew immediately what he had done and looked in horror – he had simply got carried away in the excitement of the moment. I have seen pickers-up survive similar narrow squeaks on several occasions,

and unfortunately I have several times looked down the wrong end of a set of barrels while actually standing in the line.

To rely on a safety catch when carrying a loaded gun is inviting trouble. A safety catch is a simple mechanical device which is always liable either to malfunction or to be accidentally knocked 'off'. And carrying a loaded gun

Don't hold your gun so that it points at your neighbour! Obvious advice, but often overlooked.

is unforgivable unless actually walking-up. This situation calls for extreme care – before every shot is taken you must ask yourself, 'Is it safe?'. There have been so many accidents, many tragic, in these circumstances.

The rule of never having a loaded gun other than when about to shoot is also applicable when crossing fences or gates. You may do everything absolutely correctly, with the barrels pointing skywards at all times, but what if you lost your footing? It has happened before, and will happen again. Break your gun, remove the cartridges (on a driven day this will have been done already) and pass the gun to a friend on the other side of the fence, ditch or whatever.

When actually shooting or waiting to shoot it is a good idea to remember 'Heaven' and 'Hell' – keep the barrels pointing at either one or the other, sky or earth. Certainly don't carry your gun sideways on your arm – it will point at your neighbour.

The most common disregard for safety is that of people on formal driven days who insist on keeping their guns closed at all times. They may have removed the cartridges, but no one else can be sure of that. It is disturbing to be in such company, for no matter how experienced these shots are, we are all human and prone to forgetfulness. They might as well be carrying a semi-automatic, the very gun which they would probably frown upon.

Finally, it is a good idea to keep checking that your barrels are clear. A bit of mud or dirt could easily cause a barrel blockage and have disastrous consequences. Similarly, I remember once having what sounded like a misfire, and yet the cartridge ejected normally. There were five mallard overhead at the time, and I was just about to go for a right and left – but something didn't seem quite right. Smoke hung from the breech. Rather than reload, I quickly checked and found that a wad had jammed up the barrel. If I had reloaded and pulled the trigger I would most likely have burst the barrel and suffered terrible injuries as a result.

Why shouldn't you carry both 12 and 20 bore cartridges? A 20 bore shell slipped into a 12 bore chamber will slip down the barrel. In an absent-minded moment, a 12 bore cartridge could be loaded on top of it. I needn't add what would follow, other than that a spell of absent-mindedness could cost a life.

One other area that is worthy of attention is the buying of second-hand guns, particularly older guns. Have they been properly vetted and are they still in proof? The shooting world is full of stories about thin barrel walls and faulty actions. If you have the chance of a good bargain, think twice before parting with your money. And in any event, have the gun checked before you shoot with it.

CLEANING YOUR GUN

This quite logically follows on from safety. A gun well looked after and cared for will not only maintain its price, look better and perform better, it will also be safer.

There is certainly plenty of choice of cleaning kits available at local gunshops and there is really no excuse for not cleaning a gun after every outing. While the barrels will have been cleaned with a phosphor bronze brush, a little oil should be applied to the visible working parts – but only a little. Don't overdo it. All mud and blood should be removed as quickly as possible as both are extremely corrosive, especially blood. And never, under any circumstances, leave your gun in a slip overnight. This is a particularly harmful practice in the winter when a dry gun will sweat heavily after a day in the cold. You may unzip your slip the following day to find that the blueing has been given a bit of a browning! As if by magic, rust will have taken a grip.

It is best to store the gun in a place where it can breathe, preferably a security cabinet in a room that is neither too hot nor too cold. A security cabinet itself is now an important part of the shooter's equipment. By leaving guns in places where they are easily stolen we

Check and double check that the bores are clear.

steadily rob ourselves of the opportunity to shoot. Every gun belonging to a legitimate shotgun certificate holder taken in the burglary of a house is another statistic against the existing firearms laws. It would be unbearable to discover that your favourite shotgun had been used in a violent crime. So do yourself a favour and lock it up!

CLOTHING

By some strange quirk country clothing has become widely accepted by the general public to the point where it has taken the country by storm (if you'll forgive the pun). You see people wearing shooting jackets who wouldn't know one end of a gun from the other. The acceptance of the Barbour waxed proof jacket (both home and overseas) is perhaps not too surprising, for while it has its detractors, most people are agreed that it is a good practical coat that lends itself to be worn in a whole variety of situations. In fact you rarely look out of place while wearing one anywhere these days, be it on the foreshore, the country house pheasant shoot, at the local pub or the cinema. Comfortable, light, warm waterproof – an all occasions garment.

But more recently there have been other options that have also caught on in a big way. The lightweight goretex garment that brought its makers name Schoffel to our attention, and is now available in other makes, became a big hit in shooting circles. Though more expensive than waxproof it lent itself well to the shooting field. Simultaneously, at around the same time and price, there became available a whole variety of tweed shooting coats, invariably goretex lined. And very attractive too.

Though there are some who argue that a good old fashioned tweed shooting jacket, as part of the shooting suit, takes some beating. I have a friend who wears nothing else whilst shooting, and it seems to carry any amount of rain, yet he never gets wet.

It is a matter of preference and finding a garment to match your budget – the key considerations are 'does it fit and is it practical?'. It will need to keep you warm and dry, but offer enough room to enable you to shoot in comfort. Some coats are far too tight at the shoulder.

Leggings, love them or loathe them, are also an undoubted asset. There is always a time during a season when you will be glad of them, and not only do they cut out the rain, they also keep out the cold.

Wellingtons (green or black!) are without doubt the greatest essential for all who shoot. Some prefer boots or maybe stout leather shoes with breeks, but again the prime consideration is whether your footwear is practical. Breeks themselves are, in fact, an ideal alternative to trousers. They are comfortable, offer room at the knee and, with a good pair of strong socks, are also surprisingly warm.

Head gear is another must, be it cap, deerstalker or trilby. The advantage of a rimmed hat is that water which runs off the back will clear your neck. In the middle of a storm it's bad enough getting hands and face wet, but when it starts to drip down your neck then you've really got trouble. A band around a hat also offers a gallery for your collection of woodcock pin feathers. And a rim allows better camouflage, which is necessary for driven game shooting as well as pigeon. Game don't like the look of a big white face staring at them any more than pigeon. This is particularly so with grouse – don't give all the shooting to the next chap. Having said all that, I mostly wear a cap!

A cravat or choker is also a useful item to own, another garment to keep you both warm and dry. And, of course, a pair of gloves which are warm but practical. Fingerless mittens are quite good, but once fingertips get cold it's jolly hard to get them warm again. Shooting gloves are available, with a slit to allow a trigger finger to poke through. These are very sensible. Some prefer black leather gloves. You make your own decision, but always give thought to your trigger finger – you will want

A range of sporting clothing, left to right: tweed suit, Gore-tex jacket, waxed coat and quilted coat.

to pull the trigger as and when needed, and you will most definitely not wish to fire the gun by accident. Cold hands or heavily gloved hands are quite capable of such mishaps.

Quilted jackets have been very popular. They are both light and warm and are ideal for fine weather shooting. A quilted vest can double up nicely as an insulating garment underneath a Barbour where its lack of bulk is an additional benefit.

An interesting aspect of shooting garments is that most shooters either wear Barbour, Goretex or a good old-fashioned shooting suit. These were once new fashions and were very

popular as such. Nowadays the newer ideas come from the continent, where dress is at its most elegant. There is some fabulous French and Austrian sporting clothing, but though I like that style of dress very much, I'll have to admit to being as dyed-in-the-wool as the next man!

You get attached to odd items of clothing – a favourite old coat or hat. You often see people wearing hats in conditions close to that of a mechanic's rag or maybe falling apart at the seams. The hat carries all the memories – it is also the lucky hat. Each woodcock pin feather tells its own story.

But though you want to wear your favourite old clothes, and it's good to wear colours that are akin to camouflage, you will also want to be presentable. Whether you are a guest on a pheasant shoot or asking for permission to shoot some pigeons, the way you look will affect your day. And if you look good, you very often feel good. Confidence is everything.

ACCESSORIES

Part of the fun of shooting is putting together a never-ending collection of knick-knacks, but certain accessories are essential.

At the top of the list is a cartridge bag. Buy a good, strong leather bag – it will last years and become a faithful companion. Many shooters seem to like a cartridge belt. The one situation where they are useful is in duck, grouse or partridge shooting on a warm day or evening, but otherwise I am not a great fan. I find it awkward to remove cartridges in a hurry and they can give your stock a nasty scratch (that perhaps is down more to the owner than to the belt). They do have their moments, though, so it's perhaps worth getting one. A good gun slip and maybe a gun case will also go on the shopping list, plus a decent knife and a game bag.

These are the real essentials. Thereafter the list is endless – shooting stick, torch, flasks (hip and coffee), cleaning equipment, plus an endless array of paraphernalia for the pigeon and duck shooter, not to mention dog owner. You may also wish to consider some form of hearing protection. Admittedly there are some situations when you will want to hear everything, be it an approaching bird or someone else shouting, but for the remainder it will be worth taking precautions against deafness, with either muffs or plugs. Lost hearing is never restored.

Another useful addition is a game priest. The Game Conservancy Trust market one of these and they are an extremely useful item. While everyone who shoots game should make a point of learning how to despatch any wounded quarry quickly, this is not always so easy and a priest makes clean light work of what can sometimes be an awkward job. One of the nice points of being interested in shooting is that choosing Christmas gifts is seldom a problem for family and friends.

LESSONS

There is nothing like practice and everyone who shoots game will benefit from a lesson every now and again. Good habits have a knack of giving way to bad and only an instructor will be able to detect your waywardness. Similarly, no one can hope to shoot well at the start of the season without some practice. It will take a bit of shooting to iron out the rough spots, and by that time you may have made a hash of some potentially super shooting. David Olive is a marvellous coach and I have seen him transform indifferent shots into very good ones at his Apsley Shooting School, near Andover.

There is now no shortage of shooting grounds around the country and a local gun club is another place that may be worth a visit. It doesn't matter that you may shoot 30 sporting clays, none bearing any resemblance to a pheasant, it is the familiarity of gun handling that is important. In any event, mastering some of the more awkward shots on the layout is a sure way of getting in the groove for the new season.

A lesson is always an excellent idea, but make sure of visiting a coach who has been recommended by shooting colleagues who have benefited from his tuition.

LICENSED TO SHOOT

Without wishing to state the obvious, anyone reading this book is almost certain to be the holder of a shotgun certificate, but how many hold game licences? Available from the Post Office, it would appear that a declining number of sportsmen bother to buy one. Yet more checks are being made on shoots and it would be very embarrassing to have to appear before the local magistrates for the sake of parting with a relatively small sum of money.

ON THE TABLE

All species included in this book have one thing in common – they make excellent eating. 'Don't shoot it if you can't eat it' is a perfect sportsman's guideline (allowing a shell or two for vermin). My own particular favourite is partridge. Others prefer duck or maybe snipe, woodcock, jugged hare or pigeon pie. And grouse is sold for exorbitant prices in West End restaurants.

There is also no denying that the pheasant takes some beating, both for the amount of meat on its bones and the quality of it. There is much talk about leaving pheasants to hang, though those who prefer a well-hung bird of two weeks or so are mostly those who don't have to pluck them! In warmish winter weather I would tend to pluck a bird fairly soon after getting it home, and despite being quick off the mark, I haven't noticed that the taste or texture suffers too badly as a consequence (apologies for the heresy).

Appendix

ASSOCIATIONS

Every shooting man worth his salt should belong to at least one of the associations. There are three main bodies to which the game shot will turn his attention – The British Association of Shooting and Conservation (better known as BASC), The Game Conservancy Trust and the Countryside Alliance (formerly known as the British Field Sports Society). Until we all voluntarily belong to one of these bodies, the non-shooting world will not be aware of the strength of our numbers. A heavily subscribed membership of the associations is vital as it is otherwise impossible for our case to be presented to the legislators, and much extremely important research work on game and wildlife cannot be undertaken.

The Game Conservancy Trust

Membership (25,000) largely constitutes the more serious game shots (predominately driven) and particularly shoot owners. The Game Conservancy Trust is a charitable trust which works mostly as a research body with a large team of scientists undertaking much valuable work on all game species, and also offers an important advisory service to shoots all around the country. Their results have also shown increasing evidence of the important role that shooting is playing in our environment. A habitat for game is a habitat for all wildlife. A very important message is being put across. For details, write to: The Game Conservancy Trust, Fordingbridge, Hampshire. SP6 1EF. Tel. 01425 652381. www.gct.org.uk

The BASC

With a membership of 120,000 this association covers all quarry shooting. Founded in 1908 as WAGBI (Wildfowlers of Great Britain and Ireland), it has blossomed into an active representative body for the sport. For their membership fee, members also receive insurance cover and a quarterly magazine *Shooting and Conservation*. It maintains a busy promotional programme, with widespread outside events in the summer and an increasing number of roadshows around Britain on winter evenings. It also undertakes much political, legal, advisory and research work and offers assistance to members in all three areas. For details, write to: The BASC, Marford Mill, Rossett, Wrexham LL12 0HL. Tel. 01244 573000. www.basc.org.uk.

The Countryside Alliance

With a membership of 100,000, this organisation is different from the other two, since it concentrates much more on the political aspects of campaigners for hunting, shooting, fishing and coursing. With hunting and coursing under its wing it very often comes in for sharp attacks. Increasingly high profile, it also initiates much important work undertaken behind the scenes on our behalf. It has latterly been at the forefront of the big political debate to ban hunting. But it also runs the Campaign for Shooting and SOS (Save our Sport) fundraiser, and has a quarterly magazine *Campaign Update*. For details, write to: The Countryside Alliance, The Old Town Hall, 367 Kennington Road, London SE11 4PT. Tel. 020 7840 9200. www.countryside-alliance.org

All of these organisations need our support, and every shooting man should belong to at least one of them. Here endeth the lesson!

Shooting Season

While certain dates on the shooting calendar are known and remembered by all who shoot, there are certain anomalies and it is worth while keeping all relevant dates at the back of your mind. All of the dates quoted are inclusive.

Grouse: 12 August–10 December

Ptarmigan: 12 August–10 December

Snipe: 12 August–31 January

Black game: 20 August–10 December

Wild duck and geese: 1 September–31 January; in or over areas below the high water mark of ordinary spring tides, 1 September–20 February

Golden plover: 1 September–31 January

Coot and moorhen: 1 September–31 January

Partridge: 1 September–1 February

Pheasant: 1 October–1 February

Woodcock: 1 October–31 January; in Scotland, 1 September–31 January

Pigeon and rabbit: no close season

Hare: no close season, but on moorlands and unenclosed non-arable lands may be shot only by the occupier and authorised persons 11 December–31 March.

The various species of wild duck and geese on the quarry list are:

Duck: mallard, teal, wigeon, pintail, common pochard, gadwall, shoveller, tufted, common scoter, garganey teal, goldeneye, long-tailed, scaup-duck, velvet scoter.

Geese: Canada, greylag, pink-footed, white-fronted. There is limited shooting of barnacle geese on the Isle of Islay.

Be careful over the closing dates of the seasons. Due to anomalies which have arisen as a result of mergers of different game, wildlife and protection of birds acts, we now have a situation where it is perfectly legal to shoot partridge and pheasant on 1 February but no other species (unless below the high water mark). A woodcock or a teal on an end of season shoot can offer a very tempting shot, but think twice.

It is also generally agreed that both the partridge and pheasant seasons start almost a month too early. It matters little, for few people shoot partridges in September or pheasants in October. Birds are seldom mature enough to be considered a serious sporting proposition during these months.

Further Reading

These are just a few of the many books on the subject. There is much pleasure to be had in piecing together a collection of both the old and the new on shooting related topics.

B. B. *Tide's Ending* (Hollis & Carter)
B. B. *Dark Estuary* (Hollis & Carter)
Burrard, Maj. Sir G. *Modern Shotgun*
    Vols I–III (Field Library)
Carlisle, G. L. *Grouse and Gun* (Stanley Paul)
Coats, A. *Pigeon Shooting* (André Deutsch)
Gray, N. *Woodland Management for Pheasants*
    and Wildlife (David & Charles)

Humphreys, J. *Modern Pigeon Shooting*
    (Tideline)
Martin, B. *Sporting Birds of the British Isles*
    (David & Charles)
Martin, B. *The Great Shoots* (David &
    Charles)
McKelvie, C. *Book of the Woodcock* (Debretts)
McPhail, R. *Open Season* (Airlife)
Teesdale-Buckell, *Experts on Guns and*
    Shooting (Field Library)
Thomas, G. *Shotguns and Cartridges* (A & C
    Black)

Index